DATE DUE

GAYLORD			PRINTED IN U.S.A.

The Interaction of Economics and Foreign Policy

Contributors
Richard J. Trethewey
John R. Karlik
John P. Hardt
Young C. Kim
Edward L. Morse
Fritz Bock

The Interaction of
Economics and Foreign Policy

Edited by Robert A. Bauer

University Press of Virginia
Charlottesville

THE UNIVERSITY PRESS OF VIRGINIA
Copyright © 1975 by the Kenyon Public Affairs Forum

First published 1975

Publication of this volume is sponsored by
the Kenyon Public Affairs Forum,
Kenyon College, Gambier, Ohio.
The authors alone are responsible for
the opinions expressed and the policies recommended
in their respective papers.
The Kenyon Public Affairs Forum is
a nonpartisan educational institution
and as such takes no position
on questions of public policy.

Library of Congress Cataloging in Publication Data
Main entry under title:

The Interaction of economics and foreign policy.

    Essays first presented at a Kenyon Public Affairs Forum conference in April 1974.
    1. International economic relations—Congresses. 2. International relations—
Congresses. I. Bauer, Robert A., ed. II. Kenyon Public Affairs Forum.
HF1411.I4   327   .75-2243   ISBN 0-8139-0639-3 (cloth);
ISBN 0-8139-0640-7 (paper)

Printed in the United States of America

Contents

Preface

THE essays in this volume, first presented at the Kenyon Public Affairs Forum Conference on "The Interaction of Economics and Foreign Policy," in April 1974, are by effective and recognized spokesmen of differing experiences and viewpoints. The comments and suggestions of the conference participants, whose names appear at the end of this volume, were taken into account by the authors in revising their papers. The topic is of crucial importance to international relations, and, because of the complexity of issues involved, analyses of it are necessarily incomplete.

The first essay, which presents a theoretical framework of international economics and politics, is followed by studies dealing with the impact of economic factors on the foreign policies of the United States, the Soviet Union, and Japan, and on the European Community. The final essay, by a European statesman and economic expert, reflects a general European view of the problem and presents an added perspective to the American expertise brought to bear upon the topic.

The Kenyon conference took place at a time when the special session of the United Nations General Assembly to discuss economic world problems and, particularly, the plight of developing countries heard American Secretary of State Henry Kissinger outline a six-point program of international cooperation based on a rather ominous appraisal of the international economic situation. The energy crisis, precipitated by the outbreak of fighting in the Middle East in October 1973, had demonstrated the extreme fragility of the world economy. Grave as this problem was—and is—Kissinger identified far deeper concerns: combating inflation, stimulating economic growth, supplying food to hungry and starving people in many countries, and improving the living standard of the poor. These problems have been intensified by the worldwide shortage of raw materials and compounded by the general spread of a feeling of hopelessness in man's capacity to cope with them.

The same session of the United Nations General Assembly was informed by Secretary General Kurt Waldheim that while more than 500 million human beings suffer from hunger, world food supplies have reached their lowest level in thirty years. At the same time, the world population continues to increase unchecked, and so does the arms race, on which the nations of the world spent $14 billion during the three-week special session of the General Assembly.

The arms race, the tremendous rise in oil prices since October 1973, the beginning of a vast transfer of wealth from the energy-consuming to the energy-producing countries, and "stagflation" (the new term for a stagnant and inflationary economy), to a large extent a result of the growth euphoria of the 1960s and in the United States also of the "guns and butter" policies during the Vietnam War, are some of the basic reasons for the international economic malaise. Add to this the fundamental shift from a bipolar to a multipolar political world and one can recognize the vast complex of problems facing the Western world today.

Communist countries are also increasingly involved in these developments. The Communist governments might welcome the economic disarray of the capitalist world as a confirmation of their own ideological positions and prophesies. Yet at the same time they will find themselves in a tightening economic squeeze stemming from their demands for technology transfer and for food from the Western countries. Because of the increasing trade between West and East, and the Communist countries' need to expand it further, they, too, are subject to the effects of inflationary pressures in the affluent countries.

Thus it becomes evident that the nations of the world, both rich and poor, are rapidly approaching a state of affairs that could result in the breakdown of established orders and the spread of economic and social chaos, which in turn could provoke political revolutions, civil wars, and armed conflicts between nations.

The possibility of military intervention has been discussed in connection with the protection of the uninterrupted flow of oil to the industrialized countries. Statements by high-level United States administration officials have implied that decisive actions might have to be considered should no way be found to compromise the positions of the energy-exporting and energy-consuming nations.

Grim though the preceding analysis is, the situation is not entirely hopeless. There is a promising awareness among world leaders and economists that the world's economic interdependence is such that each nation's economic policy is an integral part of its overall foreign policy and has a greater impact than ever on other countries. Efforts to solve unemployment problems in one country can cause workers to lose jobs in another. Attempts to ease inflationary pressures by tightening the money supply in one country can be severely hampered by a large influx of interest-sensitive foreign capital.

The energy problem concerns all nations. Producing countries cannot prosper if consuming countries falter. It is no longer possible for a country to assert absolute sovereignty over its domestic economy without affecting the welfare of other nations. Negotiation and cooperation, not confrontation, must constitute the answer to the problems.

This volume is presented as a contribution to the intensive debate in international, governmental, financial, and academic circles that must produce both short- and long-term solutions to this, the overriding challenge of our days. As Pericles of Athens said in about 430 B.C., "Although only a few may originate a policy, we are all able to judge." More than ever before, the conduct of international foreign and economic affairs is very citizen's business, for such matters have a decisive impact on the livelihood and economic well-being of individuals, as well as on the domestic stability of nations and the possibility of world peace.

ROBERT A. BAUER

The Interaction of Economics and Foreign Policy

International Economics and Politics
A Theoretical Framework

Richard J. Trethewey

THE past few years have witnessed the increasing involvement of economic issues in the world of high international diplomacy, issues that had formerly been resolved at a lower level of foreign policy decision-making. As Richard Cooper notes, "Historically trade issues frequently intruded into, and occasionally even dominated, high foreign policy among countries. But this intrusion was successfully suspended during the past twenty-five years by postwar agreements, notably the Bretton Woods Agreement and the General Agreement on Tariffs."[1] With the ending of the postwar economic order, trade issues have left their lower track to become part of "high foreign policy." Economic problems such as the effects of international corporations, cartelization of exporting countries, barriers to trade, and international monetary arrangements are having a major impact on world politics.

The purpose of this paper is to provide the reader with a theoretical framework for distinguishing those aspects of international relations that are economic from those that are political. The paper will explore the relationship between international economics and politics by outlining the relevant elements of trade theory and examining its relationship to political goals such as autonomy, nationalism and prestige, and foreign domination. The outcome, it is hoped, will be a workable definition of the borderline between economics and political science which will be useful and humbling to both the economist and the political scientist.

Classical International Economics and the State

The fountainhead of classical economics is to be found in Adam Smith's *Wealth of Nations*. Smith was interested in what determined

---

[1] "Trade Policy Is Foreign Policy," *Foreign Policy*, no. 9 (Winter 1972–73), pp. 18–36, reprinted in *A Reordered World: Emerging International Economic Problems*, ed. Richard Cooper (Washington, D.C.: Potomac Associates, 1973), pp. 46–47.

the income and wealth of national units, and the primary criteria
for the adoption of policy was the test of national advantage. The
consumption of the national community was to be maximized, serving
as the goal of economic activity.[2]

While Smith and the other classical economists were interested in
the national advantage, as were the mercantilists, they also pur-
ported to show that what was in the interest of one nation economically was in the interest of the others. Heavy emphasis was placed on
the desirability of widening the market through international trade
as the road to economic development and national power. The engine for economic growth was extensions in the division of labor,
which was "limited by the width of the market."[3] Growth was to be
achieved by widening the market through a reduction in internal
and external trade barriers, permitting greater specialization and
greater productivity.

The mercantilist world view was that international trade constitutes a zero sum game, in which one nation can gain only at the
expense of another. The winner is the one who captures the outflow of bullion resulting from another's unfavorable trade balance.
The world view of the classical economists was that trade is a positive
sum game, in which trade restrictions hurt each party, while free
trade benefits all nations. Thus, on these grounds Adam Smith could
recommend the end of the monopoly of the colony trade: "The
monopoly of the colony trade . . . like all the other mean, malignant
expedients of the mercantile system, depresses the industry of all
other countries but chiefly that of the colonies, without in the least

2 Lionel Robbins makes the point as follows: "It must be realized that his
consumption . . . was the consumption of a limited community, the members of
the nation state. To the extent to which they repudiated former maxims of
economic warfare and assumed mutual advantage in international exchange, it is
true that the outlook of the Classical Economists seems, and indeed is, more
spacious and pacific than that of their antagonists. But there is little evidence that
they often went beyond the test of national advantage as a criterion of policy,
still less that they were prepared to contemplate the dissolution of national
bonds. If you examine the grounds on which they recommend free trade, you
find it is always in terms of a more productive use of *national* resources." Quoted
in Roger Weiss, "Economic Nationalism in Britain in the Nineteenth Century,"
in *Economic Nationalism in Old and New States*, ed. Harry G. Johnson (Chicago:
University of Chicago Press, 1967), p. 33.

3 See Smith, *The Wealth of Nations* (New York: Random House, Modern Library Edition, 1937), pp. 3–17, for his discussion of the division of labor.

increasing, but on the contrary diminishing, that of the country in whose favor it is established."[4]

The classical economists could be both internationalists and nationalists most of the time. As Roger Weiss notes, "Fortunately, there were few instances that required Smith to have to measure the welfare of Britain against that of the rest of the world, and he was therefore able to care for both without sacrificing either."[5] The principle of free trade could be abandoned or modified for defense, for "defense is of more importance than opulence."[6] John Stuart Mill argued that the Navigation Acts were justified at the time, for Britain could not "otherwise have sufficient ships and sailors" and was thus "quite right in obtaining these means, even at an economical sacrifice in point of cheapness of transport."[7]

The classical understanding of the trade process was further refined by Ricardo through his development of the principle of comparative advantage or comparative costs. According to the analysis in *The Wealth of Nations,* a nation could increase its riches by exporting goods it produces more cheaply in exchange for goods that are produced at a lower cost abroad. Smith left the case for free trade open to the protectionist argument that since some nations may produce everything more cheaply, trade would not be advantageous.

This problem could be handled in terms of the monetary theory of trade, but not by Smith's inadequate "real" theory of trade. The problem of one nation that produces everything at a lower cost trading with other nations was resolvable in terms of Hume's specie flow mechanism. Trade would lead to an inflow of money into the country producing everything at lower prices and an outflow of money from nations producing everything at higher prices. The increased quantity of money in circulation would raise the price level, causing a substitution of imported goods for domestically produced goods and raising the price of exports. In countries experiencing an outflow of money, the price level would decline; thus the price of its exports would fall, and substitution of domestic for imported goods would result. Equilibrium would be achieved when the value

4 Ibid., pp. 567–68. Also quoted in Weiss, p. 34.

5 P. 34.

6 Smith, p. 431.

7 *Principles of Political Economy,* ed. Donald Winch (New York: Penguin, 1970), p. 281.

of exports and imports became equal through the self-correcting mechanism of a specie flow.

But the specie flow explanation does not satisfactorily explain the process of trade in real terms, that is, in terms of the factor requirements needed to produce a given commodity. Ricardo, who was the first economist to advocate that international trade be viewed as a distinct area of economics, demonstrated analytically that it was relative rather than absolute differences in cost that were crucial for trade.[8]

According to the principle of comparative advantage, a nation will become wealthier by exporting products it produces relatively more cheaply in exchange for products that can only be produced domestically at a relatively higher cost. England and Portugal can both become better off by the exchange of English cloth for Portuguese wine, despite the fact that in Ricardo's nonchauvinist example Portugal can produce both commodities more cheaply.

Viewing the process of trade through the perspective of the Ricardian model, the economist is apt to ask impatiently why nations find it so difficult to refrain from interfering with international economic transactions and thus fail to take advantage of the gains to be realized through international specialization. Having raised this question, the economist tends, in explaining the international behavior of nations, to subscribe a major role to irrational forces or a lack of information. But before granting a powerful role to irrationality or ignorance, the analyst must ask how complete the Ricardian model of international economic transactions is in view of the objectives of the nation-state.

The nation-state clearly has objectives other than the attainment of "constrained bliss," or Pareto optimality (a state where no one member of society can become better off without another member becoming worse off). Political goals such as national autonomy, nationalism, prestige, and foreign domination may be only achievable in the real world at the expense of economic efficiency. National defense, perhaps an essential prerequisite for autonomy, may require the maintenance of an industry that on economic grounds should be abandoned. Nationalism and prestige, as another example, may require controls on the international flow of capital, which can restrict

___

[8] A readily accessible treatment of Ricardian economics can be found in chapter 4 of *Economic Theory in Retrospect*, by Mark Blaugh (Homewood, Ill.: Irwin, 1968). Discussion of the Ricardian influence on trade theory can be found in any standard principles text.

economic growth and production. Foreign domination may require the underwriting of an inefficient business venture or governmental aid project abroad, while nationalism and autonomy may require limitations on the international mobility of labor.

One may properly raise the question of whether economic analysis has anything meaningful to say about the nature of these trade-offs with economic efficiency. Indeed, economists such as John K. Galbraith, Baran, and Sweezy argue that it does not. The argument of this paper is that economic analysis is highly relevant to an understanding of international processes, but that the analysis must be extended beyond classical economics and its admonition that defense is more important than affluence.

Beyond Classical International Economics

Classical international economics was able to explain neatly the gains from international trade, but only under a highly restrictive set of assumptions. From the perspective of later developments, the most important of these assumptions was that labor was the only factor of production.[9] The cost of wine and cloth production was determined solely by the necessary amount of labor time that went into their production. By viewing the process of trade through a model that specified only one factor of production, the income distribution effects of trade on national welfare were obscured.

The work of Eli Heckscher and Bertil Olin caused economists to take greater cognizance of the possibility that freer international trade might not make everyone in a society better off, something that politicians and special interest groups had long recognized. Heckscher and Olin's analysis successfully incorporated these redistribution effects into the core of international economics. The Heckscher-Olin trade theory hypothesizes that comparative advantage between

[9] There are many satisfactory treatments of modern trade theory available: Bo Södersten, *International Economics* (New York: Harper & Row, 1970), and Charles P. Kindleberger, *International Economics*, 4th ed. (Homewood, Ill.: Irwin, 1968), provide highly readable treatments for the intermediate level economics student. Delbert A. Snider, *Introduction to International Economics*, 5th ed. (Homewood, Ill.: Irwin, 1971), and Mordechai E. Krenin, *International Economics: A Policy Approach* (New York: Harcourt Brace Jovanovich, 1971), provide satisfactory but less rigorous treatments. Paperbacks available include Peter Kenen and Raymond Lubitz, *International Economics* (Englewood Cliffs, N.J.: Prentice-Hall, 1971).

nations is determined by the relative abundance of the factors of production within them.[10] Thus, a country that is abundant in labor relative to capital would have a comparative advantage in labor intensive products (those where the ratio of labor to capital is highest as determined by technology at given factor prices). A country with such a comparative advantage would, upon the opening up of its economy, export labor intensive products in exchange for capital intensive products.

The country with a relative abundance of capital would experience comparative advantage in capital intensive products, exporting them in exchange for labor intensive products. This is not very different from what the Ricardian model specifies, in that relative costs determine comparative advantage and trade. However, it has the very important property of specifying the resulting change in the distribution of income. As the labor intensive country exports its labor intensive products, the wage is bid up, while the price of capital falls. Total income is greater, labor is better off, but capital holders are worse off. The effect of trade is to redistribute income both relatively and absolutely in favor of labor.

In the capital intensive country, where capital intensive products are exported in exchange for labor intensive products, the effect of income distribution is just the opposite. The exportation of those products leads to more of the capital intensive goods being produced, and less of the labor intensive products being produced. The price of capital is bid up, while the price of labor falls. Thus, the capital intensive country experiences a gain in income, and an absolute and relative redistribution of income in favor of capital owners.

Specialization stops when there is no further comparative advantage at the margin and the prices paid to the factors of production are the same across national boundaries. Hence, free movements of products across borders is a substitute for perfect factor mobility. Empirical verification of the Heckscher-Olin trade theory has proved difficult for a number of reasons, resulting in the famous "Leontiff Paradox."[11] But the theory introduced distributional effects into the

---

10 Eli F. Heckscher was a Swedish economist and economic historian equally well known for his studies on mercantilism and Swedish economic history. The core of the Heckscher-Olin trade theory appeared in a seminal paper he wrote in 1919. Bertil Olin, a Swedish economist and politician, was a student of Heckscher's. His *Interregional and International Trade* was published in 1933.

11 For a discussion of factor reversal and the Leontiff Paradox, see Södersten, chap. 7.

core of international economic analysis and consequently into the economist's world view. No longer could the possible redistribution of welfare resulting from international economic transactions be ignored.

The first-best solution to the distribution problem is the compensation principle of modern welfare economics. The economist could maintain the essential elements of the classical view of trade by advocating compensation for the losers from increased international trade. The net gains in trade would permit the losers to be compensated with money, with the result that the nation and the world would be unambiguously better off through increased economic efficiency.

This extension of trade theory enables economists to analyze obstacles to freer international trade within the realm of the rational as second-best solutions to particular distribution goals of segments of society. Economic analysis can rationally interpret compensation schemes such as the Common Market's Common Agricultural Policy or the retraining provisions of the American Trade Expansion Act as politically possible means to prevent the realization of distribution goals through even less efficient means.

The compensation principle does bring us to the borderline between political science and economics. On distribution grounds per se, there is not a conflict between economics and politics, although there may be a conflict for a particular scheme. Redistribution schemes that are politically acceptable are typically second-best solutions economically, in that they introduce additional inefficiencies in the process of removing larger inefficiencies. For example, the politically acceptable compensation for an area that has been displaced by freer international trade may be to redevelop the area, while on economic grounds it should be abandoned. The compensation scheme itself can introduce additional inefficiencies that will partially or perhaps completely offset the gains from freer trade.

Economic analysis can only tell if the second-best solution is making the country economically better or worse off, but it cannot explain what makes a second-best solution preferable to a best solution. At that point the process is essentially political rather than economic. Although the economist typically does not see the first-best solution of cash subsidies for losers realized, he can still advise the politician which politically acceptable scheme is second-best as opposed to third-best.

Modern analysis has also opened up other possibilities for explaining political intervention in the world of international economic transactions. The theory of international prices shows that it is possible under certain conditions to alter the terms of trade favorably through the use of an "optimum tariff" and/or export taxes. The prescription of classical trade theory rested on the assumption of pure competition for individuals, firms, and nations. Under pure competition, buyers facing supply curves that are perfectly elastic are price takers. Sellers facing demand curves that are perfectly elastic are also price takers. Such an assumption is realistic on the individual or firm basis when the amount any one individual buys or any firm sells is a small part of the total amount bought and sold on the market. It is realistic for a nation if the nation's imports or exports of a product are a small part of the total world trade in that commodity.

Modern trade theory shows that when a nation buys enough of a product from abroad, or sells enough of it on the world market so that the nation is no longer a price taker, the terms of trade can be improved by imposing a tax on the product. As a practical matter this has never been important in the case of imports, but it is becoming more important in the case of exports.[12] Here the state or states impose a cartel, permitting a higher price to be charged on the world market. American-trained Arab economists have been advising Organization of Petroleum Exporting Countries (OPEC) and are thoroughly familiar with the analysis.

Economists have yet to develop a generally accepted model of market behavior under cartel arrangements, but there are a few generally accepted principles that have come out of the attempts. Cartels tend to be highly unstable arrangements, often breaking down in the face of declining demand or a reduction in the rate of increase in demand. The end of the oil boycott on America may have been essential for maintaining the high price of Middle East crude oil. We also know that the greater the number of members in a cartel, and the greater the difference between price and marginal cost, the more likely it is that the cartel will be unstable. Given the large number of alternative sources of supply for all commodities except oil, such cartel arrangements are unlikely to pose greater international economic and political problems than they do at present. With regard

[12] Charles P. Kindleberger makes the point that tariffs are used in fact to raise revenue rather than to alter the terms of trade. See Kindleberger, *Power and Money* (New York: Basic Books, 1970), pp. 127–28.

to oil, the current ratio of price to marginal cost at the Persian Gulf is roughly seventy to one, which is probably far too great a difference to be maintainable.

International Economics, Autonomy, and Development

Within a static context the requirements for international economic efficiency do place constraints on political policy, but they are not inordinately severe. Even such nationalistic political goals as autonomy and cultural identity are not totally incompatible with economic efficiency. Autonomy and cultural identity have led the modern state to place restrictions on the immigration of labor in the twentieth century. It is interesting to note that Ricardo urged that international economics be a separate branch of economics because of the immobility of capital, not labor.[13] The work of Heckscher and Olin demonstrates that trade in products can substitute to a large extent for factor mobility across national borders. Indeed, the existence of reasonably free capital mobility and product mobility will give nearly the same result as would be achieved with free labor mobility.

An example of this process can be seen in the market response to restrictions on the importation of Mexican workers into the United States. For reasons of autonomous national goals, the U.S. government severely restricted the inflow of Mexican workers, perhaps because poverty is less of a problem when it is outside one's own borders. The market response has been an outflow of capital, providing employment in Mexico for these workers who were formerly crossing over to work in the American economy.

National defense may not be compatible with the maximization of private affluence, but it is not inherently incompatible with economic efficiency. Consider the case of one of the so-called vital industries, steel. Assume that policymakers view a certain level of capacity in this industry as essential for national defense, yet under free competition it will not be provided because of the importation of foreign steel. Within this context capacity to produce steel becomes a public good, which in principle can be provided for by a governmental action fully compatible with economic efficiency.

The economically correct way to achieve this level of capacity is with a lump-sum government subsidy to the industry, which would

13 Blaugh, p. 126.

show the taxpayer directly how much defense is costing. The subsidy should not result in a subsidy to steel users as such, since it is steel production that is generating the external benefits, not steel consumption. Not only does the subsidy have the advantage of making known the cost of defense, but defense is being paid for according to one's general tax contribution.

A second- or third-best way, and perhaps the politically most acceptable way, is to acquire the needed level of capacity by placing a tariff on steel imports. This method would cost society more than the subsidy, due to the misallocation of resources caused by the higher price paid for steel and the higher marginal costs of domestic steel production.[14] In addition, people with a greater preference for steel consumption would pay a disproportionate amount of the defense budget, and the costs of defense would be hidden from the public.

It may be the case politically that hidden subsidies are to be preferred to open subsidies; and on paternalistic grounds one may argue that people will tend to spend too little for defense anyway, so it is best that the costs be hidden. These are clearly noneconomic arguments; all economic analysis can do is point out the difference in costs between first- and second-best solutions. The political process will have to decide if the nation can afford that difference.

The above cases are fundamentally static situations, where the allocation of resources is examined for a given moment in time. Within a dynamic context the difference between first- and second-best solutions presents a formidable problem for both political and economic analysis. For autonomy to be achieved in the twentieth century, some degree of economic development is essential. Yet it has been suggested by some analysts that an efficient allocation of resources according to the principle of comparative advantage is not compatible with economic development, particularly for so-called Third World countries. Neo-Marxists such as Baran, Sweezy, and Frank argue that trade, as determined by comparative advantage with the developed world, dooms these countries to permanent underdevelopment.[15] They advocate a planned economy in which the state would regulate and determine international trade.

[14] For a discussion of the distortions caused by the use of tariffs rather than subsidies, see Harry Johnson, "Tariffs and Economic Development: Some Theoretical Issues," *Journal of Developmental Studies* 1, no. 1 (Oct. 1964):3–30. Also available in Bobbs-Merrill Reprint Series in Economics, Econ-159.

[15] The following all present this interpretation: Paul A. Baran, *The Political*

Less radical economists such as Ragnar Nurske have made similar criticisms of trade patterns resulting from the dictates of the market and advocate a major role for government in overseeing trade relations. Nurske argues as follows:

> In the absence of a vigorously upward-shifting world demand for exports of primary products, a low-income country through a process of diversified growth can seek to bring about upward shifts in the domestic demand schedules by means of increased productivity and therefore increased purchasing power. In this way a pattern of mutually supporting investments in different lines of production can enlarge the size of the market and help to fill the vacuum in the domestic economy of low-income areas.[16]

According to Nurske, the classical prescription of increased trade through comparative advantage was an engine for growth in the nineteenth century. But in the twentieth century, with the slowing down in the growth of demand for primary products owing to the development of synthetic substitutes and the low income-elasticity of demand, such trade is unlikely to transmit growth.[17] Further, the resulting trade pattern leads to overspecialization.[18] Selective state interference is recommended to achieve a needed balanced growth path.[19]

Nurske's argument, however, is less a demonstration of the incompatibility of static efficiency according to the principles of comparative advantage than it is a confusion of first- and second-best solutions to the correct allocation of resources. If the too exclusive exporting of primary products limits growth, it follows that there must be an externality involved or a lack of information.[20] If the terms of trade are, over time, turning against primary products, the individual entrepreneur with this information will adjust his investments accordingly, internalizing the benefits and costs. But if there are exter-

---

Economy of Growth (New York: Monthly Review, 1957); Baran and Paul M. Sweezy, *Monopoly Capital* (New York: Monthly Review, 1966); André Gunder Frank, *Latin America: Underdevelopment or Revolution* (New York: Monthly Review, 1969).

16 Nurske, "International Trade Theory and Development Policy," in *Economic Development for Latin America*, ed. Howard Ellis and Henry Wallich (New York: St. Martin, 1961), chap. 9. Also available in Bobbs-Merrill Reprint Series in Economics, Econ-240, p. 245.

17 Econ-240, p. 244.

18 Ibid., pp. 250–59.

19 Ibid., pp. 245–59.

20 Johnson, pp. 3–11.

nalities involved, as is sometimes argued in the case of the infant industry, an optimal investment allocation will not be forthcoming. The correct and first-best solution is to subsidize the externality, which may be accomplished, for instance, through lower taxes.[21]

Restrictions on trade are clearly second-best approximations to the correct solution, which can only be justified on political grounds. But even for the second-best solution to result in an improved allocation of resources, the economist must be relied on. Johnson notes:

> The fundamental problem is that, as with all second-best arguments, determination of the conditions under which a second-best policy actually leads to an improvement of social welfare requires theoretical and empirical investigation by a first-best economist. Unfortunately, policy is generally formulated by fourth-best economists and administered by third-best economists; it is therefore very unlikely that a second-best welfare optimum will result from policies based on second-best arguments.[22]

International economic analysis is in fact compatible with the optimum achievement of economic growth in a given institutional setting. But growth theory is not development theory, for development theory seeks to explain the determination of alternative institutional settings that will generate alternative growth paths. There is far less agreement about development theory than about growth theory.

This leads to a very important area of conflict between the analysis of trade and the analysis of development; it may be that selective interference with the market mechanism internationally and domestically is the politically feasible way to achieve an institutional framework conducive to growth. Economists are reaching the point where a meaningful specification of such an environment is possible. North and Thomas define it as follows:

> Growth will simply not occur unless the existing economic organization is efficient. Individuals must be lured by incentives to undertake socially desirable activities. Some mechanism must be devised to bring social and private rates of return into closer parity. Private benefits or costs are the gains or losses to an individual participant in any economic transaction. Social benefits or costs are those affecting the whole society. A discrepancy between private and social benefits or costs means that some third party or

21 Ibid., pp. 11–12.
22 Harry G. Johnson, "The Efficiency and Welfare Implications of the International Corporation," in *The International Corporation: A Symposium*, ed. Charles P. Kindleberger (Cambridge, Mass.: M.I.T. Press, 1970), p. 56.

parties, without their consent, will receive some of the benefits or incur some of the costs. Such a difference occurs whenever property rights are poorly defined, or are not enforced. If the private costs exceed the private benefits individuals ordinarily will not be willing to undertake the activity even though it is socially profitable.[23]

In the absence of a system of moral incentives, such as those being seriously experimented with in China, the institutional framework that will generate growth must bring about an approximate equality between social and private benefits or costs. As an example of this problem, consider the following institutional arrangement, which is typical of underdeveloped countries. There is a ceiling on interest charges paid by borrowers or to savers by financial intermediaries. Since the rate of inflation in the economy exceeds this money rate of interest, the real rate of interest is negative. The private act of saving has a positive social benefit, assuming realistically that the marginal physical product of capital is positive; but the private benefit is negative, since, owing to inflation, the interest paid is less than the depreciation in the value of the principal. As a result, little or no savings would take place through financial intermediaries, and consequently there would be only very modest capital formation and a low rate of growth.

This was the case in Brazil prior to the military takeover. The new government slowed down the annual rate of inflation from over 100 percent to 12 percent by reducing the growth rate of the money supply. The money rate of interest was allowed to rise, and inflation-proof bonds were legally permitted and encouraged. The result was to bring an approximate equality between the social and private benefits of savings. Since individuals could then benefit by the socially desirable act of saving, capital formation went up and the growth rate soared to over 10 percent per year.

As noted, economists have been able to develop models that specify alternative institutional arrangements for achieving economic growth, but neither economists nor political scientists have been able to develop a satisfactory general theory of how societies develop institutional frameworks. An economist analyzing a problem such as the international corporation's role in underdeveloped countries may tend to overlook the relationship between given policies and

[23] Douglass C. North and Robert P. Thomas, *The Rise of the Western World: A New Economic History* (New York: Cambridge University Press, 1973), p. 2-3.

the development process. Policies that may appear, within a narrow context, to be retarding growth may, within a broader developmental context, be aiding growth by creating a more prosperous and numerous middle class and more stable institutions. Nationalism and prestige may be essential to this process and yet may result in policies that seem to limit growth rather than encourage it.

The international corporation, for instance, aids the process of growth by supplying underdeveloped nations with superior technology, capital, and managerial ability. Yet too heavy a reliance on the international corporation as the engine for economic growth may hinder institutional development that is conducive to growth in the long run. If the international corporation is relied on for capital formation, less political pressure may be generated to develop an efficient domestic capital market. Relying on the international corporation for managers may substantially restrict the entry of nationals into the middle class and limit the pressure for greater investment in human capital.

Harry Johnson points out that nationalism is a type of public good which, like any public good, can be acquired at the expense of producing less of other goods in the economy.[24] What we know very little about, unfortunately, is the return to society from this type of investment. "The economist cannot in principle dispute the public taste, though he can question whether the policies adopted are well designed to secure their ostensible objectives, and can stress the need for examination of alternative methods of securing these objectives."[25]

One method of producing nationalism is the complete or partial nationalization of foreign enterprises. This action at the same time subsidizes the middle class, because the increased hiring of inferior quality nationals raises the costs of production.[26] This in turn may increase the stability of a middle-class-oriented regime or create pressures for change that will foster the interests of the middle class. The reduced inflow of technology, capital, and management, and the increased production costs, may be more than offset by a favorable improvement in the institutional framework of society.

---

[24] Johnson, "A Theoretical Model of Economic Nationalism in New and Developing States," *Political Science Quarterly* 80, no. 2 (June 1965):169–85, reprinted in *Economic Nationalism in Old and New States*, pp. 1–16.

[25] Johnson, "Efficiency and Welfare," pp. 49–60.

[26] Johnson, "Theoretical Model," pp. 10–11.

Insofar as attempts to interfere with economic transactions, as in Mexico, Peru, or Brazil, may be furthering institutional development conducive to growth in some cases, the economist cannot label all such activity as falling exclusively within the province of the political. The benefits of the international corporation can be captured at least partially under very restrictive conditions, as has been demonstrated in Mexico.

In the developed non-Communist world the response to the international corporation has been largely political. Thus, French politician and journalist Servan-Schreiber is worried about American domination of Europe through the international corporation, although the growth rate of the European economy and that of European corporations exceed the growth of the American economy and that of American corporations. This type of concern over nationalism and prestige is difficult to envision—even in an economic context—as falling within the bounds of rational economic behavior, except that it represents the production of nationalism as a pure consumer public good.[27]

Governmental dissatisfaction with the international corporation, in my view, is more basically a dislike for and misunderstanding of the operation of the marketplace. Domestically, governments are everywhere baffled by the response of the marketplace. William Simon, when he was the federal energy chief, could not understand why more crude oil was not being refined when there was no incentive to do so. The British government cannot understand why landlords do not keep their property in good repair when their rents have been frozen, in some cases for decades. The United States government cannot understand why there has been no expansion in paper-producing capacity, which is clearly needed, since the price freeze of 1971. The marketplace simply does not give planners the results they want, such as reduced inflation and at the same time lower unemployment.

Government and people are particularly perturbed when it is a foreign corporation that is the market vehicle for giving them the results they do not fully like. The international corporation follows the dictates of the market and earns the enmity of the politician, but the real problem is the market itself. When the international corporations converted dollars into marks, they were not creating the

27 Johnson, "Efficiency and Welfare," p. 50.

dollar crisis, as some critics suggest. They were responding to market forces that indicated the dollar was overvalued.

The political machinations of international corporations provide a well-known list of horror stories: bribing of tax officials, interference in foreign elections, and so on. The role of the international oil companies has been, and still is, heavily political. A fresh crop of horror stories is likely to come out of the Arab oil boycott, particularly as regards the treatment of the Japanese by the oil companies. These types of problems are manageable by legislation for the most part and in my view, do not constitute the heart of the problem.

It is the market activities of the international corporation that constitute the essence of the problem and restrict the autonomy of nations. It is conceded that most international corporations behave better politically in their host countries than their domestic counterparts do;[28] yet they prove to be more frustrating because they are foreign and because they may restrict some elements of autonomy more than noninternational corporations and companies.

The international corporation has flexibility that enables it to shift production across borders. Politicians will be unhappy facing this flexibility when it limits the power of the government to tax a given industry. Governments and unions will be frustrated when strikes or large wage increases lead an international company to shift production from one country to another. The company follows the dictates of the market; and world production is thereby increased, but the power of government and labor is reduced. The economist may well find this desirable, since it reduces the ability of government and labor to intervene in the marketplace, but politically it is very costly.

Monetary Aspects: Full Employment and International Balance

Two additional areas that involve both economic and political phenomena are full employment and international balance. Full employment, it is sometimes argued, requires a particular type of foreign policy under capitalism, while international balance heavily involves politicians and central bankers in international economic transactions.

---

[28] Carlos F. Alejandro, "Direct Foreign Investment in Latin America," in Kindleberger, *International Corporation*, p. 329.

Full Employment and Foreign Policy

An example of a fallacious economic interpretation of international politics is that it is necessary for the American government to spend large amounts of money on defense in order to assure domestic prosperity and full employment. According to this model, Keynesian unemployment is inevitable under capitalism unless there is sufficient government spending to absorb the inevitable excess of planned savings over planned investment at the full employment level of income.

Only military spending is acceptable under capitalism, according to this view, which in turn necessitates an aggressive foreign policy. Paul Baran argues as follows: "To secure popular acceptance of the armaments program, the existence of external danger has to be systematically hammered into the minds of the people. An incessant campaign of official and semiofficial propaganda, financed by both government and big business, is designed to produce an almost complete uniformity of opinion on all important issues."[29] Baran and Sweezy further argue in *Monopoly Capital* that if the military budget were cut to 1939 proportions of the GNP, "unemployment would also revert to 1939 proportions."[30]

If this economic argument were accepted as valid, according to the theoretical framework of this paper it would be a political argument to assert that compensatory government spending is necessarily military spending. In fact, it must be concluded that it is entirely political, since the economic argument is obsolete and incorrect.[31]

To get the result of an excess of planned savings over planned investment at full employment, the model assumes that there are a limited number of investment projects that will pay off under capitalism, and that most of them have already been undertaken. Even at very low rates of interest the amount of investment generated will be less than the amount of planned savings at full employment; hence, without government compensatory spending the equilibrium level of income will be below full employment.

It is further stipulated in the model that the savings rate increases

[29] Baran, p. 129.
[30] P. 176.
[31] The economic argument was developed by Alvin Hansen and was taken quite seriously by the economics profession in the late 1930s and the 1940s.

as income increases, so that as the potential income grows over time the problem of insufficient investment becomes more acute. Hence the inability of capitalism to absorb "surplus" necessitates government deficit spending to reach full employment. Only military spending is politically possible, so foreign policy must be aggressive to convince the public of the need for enormous defense budgets.

Modern economic analysis has shown the underpinnings of this scenario to be false. In the first place, it is no longer accepted that there are only a limited number of investment projects that will pay off at positive rates of interest. As the interest rate is lowered and approaches zero, the number of investment projects whose present value exceeds cost becomes nearly infinite.[32] This suggests that decreases in the interest rate through effective monetary policy can be relied on to generate full employment.

The model also incorrectly specifies the nature of the savings function, arguing that it is an increasing function of income. Modern empirical work, in this case post–World War II, has shown the savings function to be a proportional function of income over time.[33] So the economy is not faced with an ever larger proportion of savings. In addition, the argument leaves out the real balance effect, which demonstrates that the savings function could be shifted through changes in the money supply. Hence, even if it were argued that the demand for investment was inelastic on grounds of confidence, monetary policy could generate full employment.

The argument is only political and, indeed, not a very good one. Defense spending has been declining over the past two decades both as a percentage of government spending and as a percentage of the GNP. For better or worse, the public and the government clearly are willing to spend vast sums of money, which are not necessarily for full employment, on nondefense programs.[34]

32 For a discussion of secular stagnation and investment at very low rates of interest, see Robert L. Crouch, *Macroeconomics* (New York: Harcourt Brace Jovanovich, 1972), pp. 267–70.

33 See the following: J. S. Dusenberry, *Income, Savings and the Theory of Consumer Behavior* (Cambridge, Mass.: Harvard University Press, 1952); Milton Friedman, *A Theory of the Consumption Function* (New York: National Bureau of Economic Research, 1957); Modigliani and Brumber, "Utility Analysis and the Consumption Function: An Interpretation of Cross Section Data," in *Post-Keynesian Economics*, ed. Seymour Harris (New Brunswick, N.J.: Rutgers University Press, 1954).

34 In 1964, for example, defense spending was $53.6 billion, total federal spending was $118.6 billion, while the GNP was $632.4 billion. In 1973 defense

International Balance and Political Responsibility

Up to this point international economic transactions have been analyzed solely in real terms rather than in money terms. Yet an additional distinguishing characteristic of international trade, besides the restrictions on factor and product mobility, is that it involves the exchange of currencies. Unlike the domestic economy, where there is a simple exchange of money for commodities, the international economy entails an exchange of one currency for another, and then an exchange of money for the good.

If there is to be a significant and growing amount of trade internationally, there must be an institutional arrangement to facilitate the exchange of currencies. Since the transaction costs of the exchange must be minimal, the system must be able to correct surpluses and deficits in the international balance-of-payments accounts of trading nations. A failure to correct imbalances will result in the market's failing to clear, leading to high transaction costs.

To illustrate the importance of the institutional arrangement it will be useful to examine the problem of a trade deficit. A deficit occurs when, at prevailing commodity, factor, and currency prices, the amount of currency being offered for conversion into other currencies is greater than the demand for that currency by the rest of the world. The volume of money offered on the world market is determined by the value of goods and services being imported (current account) and the amount of money being invested abroad (capital account).

If a deficit on the combined current and capital account is left uncorrected, the result will be a disruption and decline in the volume of international trade. Some individuals, companies, or government agencies wanting to exchange their money for foreign currency will be unable to do so, owing to the excess supply of their own currency on the world market. Frustrated by the inability to make desired transactions, some will attempt to resolve their problem by offering a more favorable exchange rate. Buyers of that currency, fearing a change in its value as a result of the uncorrected deficit and the below-market-value currency sales, will be less willing to accept the currency at the going rate of exchange. If the exchange rate is fixed, the result will be a black market for foreign exchange, which

---

spending was $76 billion, total federal spending was $246.5 billion, while the GNP was $1,288 billion.

will increase transaction costs and thereby reduce the volume of international trade.

Nations cannot let deficits go uncorrected in view of the economic and political costs. One method for correcting a deficit is to stimulate exports and restrict imports through taxes or controls. The Labour government of Harold Wilson attempted this through an elaborate system of taxes on nonexportables and subsidies to exportables. The intent was to reduce the volume of pounds being offered on the market and, at the same time, to increase the demand for pounds.

The problem with this type of solution is that by making use of a tariff or import quota, it reduces the volume of international trade and usually results in retaliation by other nations; therefore, no net improvement in the trade balance is likely to result. Retaliation, as well as domestic distortions, will occur when the export sector is subsidized to earn additional foreign exchange. Foreign businessmen and politicians will label such a policy as "dumpng" and may subsidize their own export sector or import-competing sector to offset the trade advantage.

Controls on capital movements, although less likely to breed retaliation, are difficult to enforce and misallocate the world's supply of capital. They tend to be particularly hard on underdeveloped countries, which typically do not have well-developed domestic capital markets. The effect of the Johnson administration's controls on capital movements was very minimal in terms of the balance of payments, because a number of leaks permitted capital to find its way abroad.

The traditional method of correcting a trade deficit is to deflate the economy by increasing the size of the full-employment budget surplus and/or reducing the growth of the money supply. Exports and import-competing goods become more competitive due to their relatively lower prices. This is essentially the way deficits were corrected in the nineteenth century, when nations tied their money stocks to gold: a deficit would lead to an outflow of gold, which in turn would reduce the money supply, causing deflation.

In terms of economic welfare and national autonomy, this solution is, in the twentieth century, too costly. Prices are inflexible downward; we are faced with a short-run Phillips Curve relationship, which shows that reductions in inflation can be achieved only through increases in unemployment. Deflation reduces the rate of increase in prices, thereby increasing the real wage and causing unemployment to rise and income to fall. Such a solution drastically reduces the autonomy of a nation by imposing monetary and fiscal policies that are not always compatible with domestic employment and price policies.

The International Monetary Fund (IMF) sought to provide a solution to the market-clearing problem that would permit nations a reasonable degree of autonomy in pursuing domestic economic policy and, at the same time, would permit a significant growth in world trade.[35] Trade was to be encouraged by using a system of fixed exchange rates so as to minimize the risks of international economic transactions, and a system of central bank purchases, through the IMF, of currencies in excess supply. Long-term trade imbalance was to be corrected by a realignment of exchange rates.

The problems of international finance occurring under the IMF neatly illustrate the tension between the economically correct and the political. A brief examination of the rise and fall of the dollar will illustrate the problem.

The American dollar became overvalued on the combined current and capital account during the late 1950s, but this happened at an opportune time. The growth of world trade since World War II had been so great that a shortage of international liquidity was developing. Originally it had been envisioned that the purchases of surplus currency would be handled through the transfer of gold and a stock of foreign exchange committed to the IMF by member nations. But the value of gold and foreign exchange commitments was becoming too small in relation to the total value of world trade.

The trade deficits incurred by the United States led to an outflow of dollars; but, unlike the deficits of other nations, the American deficits were within limits welcomed by foreign central bankers. The outflow of dollars provided a solution to the liquidity problem and, in addition, gave the world an international currency. Not only could this outflow of dollars be used to finance deficits, but it could be used to finance foreign and domestic trade across the world.

The deficits were acceptable as long as they did not exceed the increases in world demand for liquidity. But in the late 1960s the deficits were becoming too large, and the United States was told, in effect, to put its house in order. It found itself in the peculiar position of having the lowest rate of inflation of all its trading partners and yet being told, particularly by the Germans and the Japanese, to reduce the deficit through deflation.

---

[35] An excellent nontechnical discussion of the IMF and the U.S. balance-of-payments deficits can be found in Kreinin.

The Bretton Woods Agreement, which established the IMF, had envisioned a world economy in which long-term deficits would be corrected by changes in the value of currencies; but, given the unforeseen prominence of the American dollar, devaluation was an unacceptable solution. A unilateral devaluation of the dollar would have induced a change in the value of virtually every other currency in the world. The consequent uncertainty and instability would have made it virtually impossible for the IMF system, as it had evolved, to remain intact.

If the system were to survive, it would be necessary for surplus-running countries, particularly Germany and Japan, to appreciate the value of their own currencies so as to reduce the size of the U.S. deficit. Yet the Japanese and the Germans balked; and, when they did appreciate, it was too little and too late. The political clout of their export and import-competing sectors was simply too great for their politicians and central bankers to overlook, keeping them from responding to the situation in an economically rational fashion. Political rationality was not compatible with the international economics of the IMF system.

As a result, when the domestic boom of 1971 caused the trade figures to show a deficit on current as well as capital accounts, convertibility was abandoned and the dollar was permitted to float in order to let supply and demand determine its value. At the same time prices and wages were frozen, and a 10-percent import surcharge was placed on imports, apparently to intimidate the Japanese and the Europeans into reducing trade barriers against American products. The Smithsonian Agreement attempted to revive the old system by formally devaluing the dollar and appreciating the yen and the mark. But the U.S. trade position did not improve dramatically enough to preserve the agreement, and in 1972 the fall of the dollar was made official as the world went essentially to a system of flexible exchange rates.

Fixed exchange rates give enormous political and economic power to central bankers and politicians, who are typically loath to see such power abandoned to the anonymous forces of the marketplace. Despite their demonstrated inability to act responsibly under a system that delegates this international economic power to them, we can expect to see continued efforts on their part to revive the old system.

There is a tension as well as a complementarity between a system of flexible exchange rates (which most academic economists favor) and political goals. While a system that relegates the authority to determine exchange values to the market reduces the power of some members of the nation-state, it actually increases the power and autonomy of others. Milton Friedman, in a classic article on flexible exchange rates, makes the point as follows:

There is scarcely a facet of international economic policy for which the implicit acceptance of a system of rigid exchange rates does not create serious and unnecessary difficulties. Promotion of rearmament, liberalization of trade, avoidance of allocations and other direct controls both internal and external, harmonization of internal monetary and fiscal policies—all these problems take on a different cast and become far easier to solve in a world of flexible exchange rates and its corollary, free convertibility of currencies.[36]

Again, however, the economist may need to heed the public taste and accept second-best solutions. Indeed, the prospect of $50 to $100 billion extra dollars of foreign exchange flowing into the Arab world may well necessitate the establishment of a revised IMF system with sufficient reserve-creating power to offset political attacks on particular currencies. This is an argument for reserve creation and not for inflexible exchange rates, although the two are likely to be equated. If such a system is established, the problem will be to recognize what is, in fact, a political attack and what is a rational economic calculus reflecting market conditions.

Conclusion

The purpose of this paper has been to provide a theoretical framework within which international economic and political phenomena can be distinguished. It is a distinctly non-Marxian framework in that it assumes that the political and the economic are substantially independent of each other and insofar as the economic analysis is largely neoclassical. Particular policies that can be shown to be incorrect on economic grounds are held to have been developed on other than exclusively economic grounds. Second- and third-best policies do have economic ramifications, and the economist can usefully advise the public or the politician on the difference in cost between these policies and best solutions. Providing better informa-

[36] "The Case for Flexible Exchange Rates" (1950), reprinted in *AEA Readings in International Economics* (Homewood, Ill.: Irwin, 1968), p. 25.

tion in these cases may well lead, subject to the constraint of public taste, to an alternative policy, but it will be arrived at through an essentially political process.

An additional and final area that illustrates the nature of the line delineating economics and politics in the real world is the problem of international environmental and resource questions. Where property rights have not been well defined, there are acute economic problems involving the overuse of resources. A classic example is the problem of fisheries.[37] Property rights over the ocean beds have not been well defined, and consequently firms within the fishing industry do not take fully into account the social cost of depletion. National policies to limit the catch are of marginal effectiveness owing to the international nature of the competition.

An optimum catch would be one where the marginal social benefits and the marginal social costs of the last unit fished would be equal. Such a catch could be estimated by a fisheries economist, but how is one to divide the catch among fishing nations? The efficient solution would be to auction the fishing rights, which would result, under profit maximization, in the most efficient firms being employed in the industry, whether they be English, Japanese, or American. But the political reality is that the correct, or first-best, economic solution is likely to be politically unacceptable to the nation that has the least-efficient fleet. The Russians would not only fear the possibility of not fishing according to their economic plan but would find the idea of an auction ideologically unacceptable. Again the economist can calculate the cost and benefits of the first-best solution, and then go on to calculate the costs and benefits of the second-, third-, and so on best solutions that may be needed to accommodate political realities.

[37] The economics is handled in H. Scott Gordon, "The Economic Theory of a Common-Property Resource: The Fishery," *Journal of Political Economy* (Apr. 1954), reprinted in *Economics of the Environment*, ed. Robert Dorfman and Nancy S. Dorfman (New York: Norton, 1972).

Economic Factors Influencing American Foreign Policy

John R. Karlik

AMERICAN foreign policy is the summation of the relationships with foreigners, including governments, established by the State Department, the Treasury Department, the Department of Defense, the president's special trade representative, the Commerce Department, the Agriculture Department, and, to a lesser extent, a number of other governmental agencies. Foreign policy is the conglomeration of what Americans in a variety of official capacities do with respect to foreigners.

Foreign Policy Goals

The actions of U.S. government representatives toward foreigners have usually sought to advance one or more of three policy goals: first, to preserve (and occasionally to expand) the territorial integrity of the United States; second, to insure that international commerce engaged in by Americans, and investments placed abroad, bear the highest possible returns or, at least, that economic competition between Americans and foreigners is conducted on more or less equal terms; and, third, to support democratic governments elsewhere in the world. To this list of idealized foreign policy goals should be added a fourth—the maintenance of stability, which invariably becomes the bureaucrat's watchword in the absence of any overriding initiative to advance one or another of the above three objectives.

Given the many departments and arms of the U.S. government that contribute to the formulation and execution of foreign policy, this policy is articulated on several different levels, not all of which are coordinated under a single overriding viewpoint or even are complementary. For example, what consular commercial officers tell American businessmen operating abroad may not always be consistent

No position stated in this paper should necessarily be construed to represent the view of any member of the Joint Economic Committee.

with policy as announced by the secretary of state. Such discrepancies may be planned or undirected. However, U.S. foreign policy comprises the totality of interactions at all levels between American government officials and foreigners.

The title of this conference, "The Interaction of Economics and Foreign Policy," implies—appropriately, I think—that the arrow from cause to effect can point in either, or both, directions. Nevertheless, during periods in the history of the United States, and even today with respect to some countries, U.S. foreign policy has been almost exclusively foreign economic policy.[1] For example, following the successful conclusion of the American Revolution, which was certainly motivated in part by a desire for economic independence, the foreign policy of the United States was primarily a foreign *economic* policy. At present, U.S. policies toward numerous developing countries and suppliers of raw materials are also primarily economic in motivation and content. A fruitful way to approach the subject is to ask to what extent economic considerations cause independent foreign policy goals to be established and to what extent these considerations impinge upon the three policy objectives specified above. Since economic issues between the Untied States and foreign countries vary substantially according to the level of development, natural resource endowment, and use of free markets in the particular foreign country considered, the analysis below considers together groups of nations with similar economic characteristics.

How Economics and Technology Can Affect
the Content and Execution of Foreign Policy

Economic circumstances can affect the formulation of and methods used to achieve foreign policy goals, including economic goals, in three major ways. *First, economic constraints may prevent the achievement of particular foreign policy objectives or may force these objectives to be redesigned on a less ambitious scale so that the economic costs of achieving them will be reduced.* Throughout most of the twentieth century, economic constraints have not seriously interfered with the achievement of U.S. foreign policy goals. During neither of

[1] For a useful discussion of this subject, see Richard N. Cooper, "Trade Policy Is Foreign Policy," *Foreign Policy*, no. 9 (Winter 1972–73), pp. 18–36, reprinted in *A Reordered World: Emerging International Economic Problems*, ed. Richard Cooper (Washington, D.C.: Potomac Associates, 1973).

the major world wars did economic costs or lack of resources force the United States to curtail its objectives. By contrast, certainly part of the opposition to U.S. involvement in Vietnam resulted from the long duration of that war and the extremely expensive manner in which it was waged. In that case, economic costs exerted a restraining influence.

Second, to achieve specific goals, economic resources may be employed in the form of largess to be distributed, sanctions to be imposed, or claims to be staked. It is standard procedure for the United States and other governments to buy favorable consideration and cooperation from foreign governments with the extension of economic and military assistance. Another tactic is to threaten the complete withdrawal of an economic benefit if another country does not modify the use of this benefit. For example, foreign exporters of steel products and textiles have been threatened with stiff statutory import quotas if the growth rate of sales to the United States was not reduced. Finally, the technological and economic capability to exploit an opportunity frequently has a strong impact in determining U.S. policy regarding its own exploitation rights versus those of other countries. No other nation has the financial and technological capability of the United States to mine minerals on and below the seabed. If the United States did not dominate in this field, its position on rights to the exploitation of the seabed 200 miles beyond its shores (still not fully defined) would probably favor international distribution of the profits from deep-sea mining more fully than it actually does.

Third, particular economic interest groups may persuade the U.S. government to adopt policies beneficial to their own narrow interests. Incidents of this type seem especially common when—as in the case of relations with developing countries—there are few military security or public policy considerations tending to curb private greed. Recent relations with Chile, Peru, and Brazil, and the history of U.S. government intervention in "banana republics" for the benefit of private American interests, demonstrate this phenomenon. On the other hand, the case of Cuba illustrates the impact of political ideology on economic relations. While disagreements over compensation for expropriated property did not help matters, the embargo on trade with Cuba was really a reaction to Premier Castro's communism and his ties with the Soviet Union. Moreover, the embargo only made payment of prompt and adequate compensation for expropriated properties more difficult.

The Relative Importance of Economic versus
Other Foreign Policy Goals

From time to time during the past few years, various senators and representatives have observed that whereas the first two or three decades following World War II were devoted to bolstering the military security of the United States and formulating political bonds among democratic governments, in the foreseeable future the over-riding emphasis will be on economic foreign policy objectives.[2] For the purposes of discussion, this issue may usefully be put in the form of a question rather than an assertion. Specifically, during the next decade or two, will economic considerations substantially influence who are the allies and opponents of the United States and the degree of support the U.S. government lends to other governments, whether democratic, authoritarian, or whatever?

To determine the likely importance of economic goals and the influence of economic considerations relative to other factors in determining U.S. foreign policy, a review is necessary of policies in the recent past and prospective future developments concerning each major economic grouping in the rest of the world. In a discussion of modest length, this review must necessarily consist of a sampling rather than an exhaustive survey.

Europe

Following World War II, the chief concern of the United States in Europe was to assure that a war among European nations would never occur again and that the countries of Western Europe would become politically and economically strong enough both to resist domestic communist parties and to provide the bulk of their own military security. While the restoration of economic health was certainly a valid aim on humanitarian grounds, from the standpoint of U.S. foreign policy European economic recovery and growth primarily constituted a means to achieve political stability under democratic governments with a high degree of military self-sufficiency.

---

[2] See, for example, U.S., Congress, Senate, Report by Sen. Abraham Ribicoff to the Committee on Finance, *A Strategy for International Trade Negotiations*, 93d Cong., 1st sess., 1973, p. 1. For a similar private view, see C. Fred Bergsten, *The Future of the International Order: An Agenda for Research* (Lexington, Mass.: D. C. Heath, 1973), pp. 1–8.

The United States sought to achieve its objectives through the extension of Marshall Plan aid, the reestablishment of multilateral trade and currency convertibility, and active encouragement of economic unification. To directly bolster the security of Western Europe against the threat of an invasion by Soviet and East European forces, the United States stationed nuclear weapons and troops overseas. While the U.S. military presence in Europe serves to achieve a military objective, the troops and material placed there represent a commitment of economic resources that have alternative uses. In this case, the United States was distributing its material largess to achieve territorial security and political objectives. Many of the reservations now expressed by Senator Mansfield and others about keeping such a large force in Europe reflect uneasiness about whether the economic costs are worth the military and political benefits.

U.S. backing for the economic unification of Europe, beginning with the European Coal and Steel Community and later expanding into a full-fledged customs union, was similarly directed, not toward an economic goal, but toward a political objective. It was reasoned that if the economies of Western Europe became closely intertwined, another war among European nations would be virtually impossible. Although this thesis may well be correct, the economies of Western Europe are still distinct national economies. Permanent tariff barriers have been abolished on the movement of most goods between European countries, but a variety of nontariff safety, health, and quality regulations still inhibit trade between members of the European Community. Moreover, an attempt to adopt a common external monetary policy, initially a joint float of European currencies with respect to the dollar, has foundered on stubborn differences regarding the conduct of domestic fiscal and monetary policies, energy policies, and assistance to backward regions.

American efforts to promote European unity have not been equal to the task. Initial U.S. advocacy was enthusiastic despite the prospect that some U.S. goods would be shut out of European markets and that, if its efforts succeeded, the United States would be building a strong competitor. In an attempt to encourage British entry into the European Economic Community (EEC), the United States, by passing the 1962 Trade Expansion Act, held out the possibility of the total abolition of tariff barriers on any item for which trade involving the United States and the EEC accounted for 80 percent or more of global trade in the item. Such a move would be meaningful only if Britain were included in the EEC, since U.S. trade with the Six accounted in only a few cases for 80 percent of world trade. Throughout the 1960s the offer of expanded access to U.S. markets had no apparent impact on French resolve to keep the British out. This negotiating authority incorporated in the Trade Expansion Act expired without being utilized.

One response on the part of U.S. business to the formation of the Common Market and to the rapid rates of economic growth that occurred in Europe during the 1960s was to leap over the tariff wall and gain access to this growing market by investing in Europe. U.S. direct investment in the six nations of the European Economic Community increased from $1.9 billion in 1959 to $15.7 billion in 1972.[3] While not a governmentally orchestrated policy, the surge of private U.S. corporate direct investment into Europe during the 1960s was a response to a perceived economic opportunity. Official policy in fact attempted to curtail the balance-of-payments outflow resulting from this investment. The controls administered by the Office of Foreign Direct Investment in the Commerce Department effectively shifted the *financing* of U.S. direct investment from the United States to Europe. But the amount of such investment was apparently reduced by only a marginal amount.

Because of the way American investment burgeoned, some Europeans became concerned about possible U.S. domination of critical sectors of European economies, especially those dependent on technological innovation for maintaining a competitive edge. Such fears have abated in Europe, perhaps because the EEC has demonstrated its ability to curb foreign takeovers of domestic firms when such actions threaten to reduce competition and because in many fields there is no alternative, at an acceptable cost, to reliance on American technology.

In coming years economic issues between the United States and Europe are certain to be important and probably will be more significant than either mutual security problems or political differences. While the threat of a Soviet invasion of Western Europe cannot be ignored, it can almost certainly be prevented by a reasonable level of preparedness on the part of European countries and, even if some troops are withdrawn, a continued U.S. commitment to defend the area. Political frictions are sure to arise from time to time, but

---

3 Estimates from U.S., Dept. of Commerce, *Survey of Current Business*, Sept. 1973, p. 24, and U.S., Dept. of Commerce, *U.S. Business Investments in Foreign Countries*, Supplement to *Survey of Current Business*, 1960, p. 89.

these differences are more likely to reflect international economic conflicts than clashes of political philosophy or *politically* motivated competition for influence in a third country.
The sharing of troop costs by the United States and European governments will undoubtedly continue to be an issue. The U.S. commitment to help defend Europe, evidenced by the location of nuclear weapons on European soil and the presence of a substantial number of Americans as both active defenders and hostages, will remain. But demands will continue to be voiced in the Congress that U.S. troops be placed in Europe only to the extent that European nations are willing to pay for maintaining them. Even if discussions with the Soviet Union on the mutual reducton of forces fail, pressure for reductions in the cost to the United States of maintaining troops abroad will linger.

The prospect of an agreement with the Soviet Union on mutual force reductions can be held out only so long. An agreement would obviously provide the mechanism for effecting troop reductions. But even in the absence of an agreement, economic forces will eventually come into play and European governments will be forced to choose between increasing their maintenance outlays or witnessing an erosion in the number of troops supplied by the United States. Here again, as with the case of Indochina, economic constraints are impinging on security considerations.

A number of particular trade disagreements exist between the United States and Europe. None of these problems is individually sufficient to provoke a major crisis, but collectively they signal general attitudes and help determine the tenor of relations. After long negotiations, American and European officials agreed on compensation for the reduction in U.S. exports resulting from British entry into the EEC. Elimination of reverse preferences that gave European exports favored access to the markets of certain African nations has apparently also removed another contentious issue between the United States and Europe.

For years the United States objected to the variable levies imposed under the Common Agricultural Policy and demanded improved access to European markets for U.S. exports of grain and meat. But the short-lived embargo imposed in June 1973 on exports of soybeans and high-protein feed substitutes has undermined the American case for access to foreign markets for agricultural products. However, U.S. reliability as a supplier should not be appreciably impaired.

The Export Administration Act, renewed in 1974, has not been substantially tightened to restrict exports of products likely to increase in price.

Beyond these specific issues, enthusiasm for the repeatedly postponed trade negotiations to reduce tariff and nontariff barriers has ebbed in both the United States and Europe. For members of the EEC, negotiations will provide the benefit of obliging them to formulate a common negotiating position with respect to the United States and their other trading partners. But these negotiations are now more frequently justified as a means of preventing the further erection of barriers to trade and of establishing a forum to contain disagreements than as a route to the dramatic elimination of trade barriers.

International monetary affairs may well be a source of continuing friction between the United States and one or more European countries. The foremost issues are likely to be the type of exchange-rate regime adopted and the official price of gold. Individuals and institutions with large volumes of liquid assets at their disposal now transfer these funds from one country to another in the event of prospective exchange-rate changes. The ability of central banks to prevent, through market intervention, exchange-rate changes that the market believes desirable has consequently been overwhelmed by the steadily growing magnitude of private funds susceptible to international transfer. Because the potency of central banks has been substantially weakened relative to private interests, fluctuating exchange rates are likely to be a continuing necessity among industrial countries. Any effort to depart substantially from this regime for rates between the United States and Europe or the United States and Japan is likely not only to produce economic maladjustments but to fail as well. Despite these realities, strong sentiments for a return to fixed rates persist, especially in some European countries.

By contrast, the adoption of fluctuating rates between the industrial countries and oil producers would be likely to have a perverse impact on the economic fortunes of the industrial nations, at least in the short run. Reserve accumulations by the oil producers imply that the value of their currencies should be increased relative to those of industrial states. But an appreciation in these currencies would produce another increase in the dollar, yen, and mark cost of oil. Since oil consumption is relatively price inelastic in the short run, the oil deficits of industrial nations would simply increase further. Thus the desire on the part of policymakers in industrial countries to maintain fixed exchange rates between their own currencies and those of the oil producers is well founded. But the existence of managed floating within the industrialized world and fixed rates with respect to the Southern Hemisphere is likely to set up tension within the monetary system. These strains will intensify calls for a return to fixed but adjustable parities—in effect, a return to the Bretton Woods system.

The Bretton Woods system had a satisfying ring of international cooperation and legitimacy to it. The members of the International Monetary Fund (IMF) were supposed to sit down and, in consultation, agree on an appropriate exchange-rate structure. The fund was equipped with sanctions against both deficit and surplus countries that failed to make appropriate exchange-rate adjustments. But in fact the system never worked as designed. Exchange-rate adjustments were unduly delayed, were excessively large and disruptive, and were biased toward devaluations rather than upward movements. The introduction of a system of fluctuating rates has replaced a philosophically well ordered regime with a much more heterogeneous one.

The joint European float against the dollar, still surviving in vestigial form, contained the possibility that two currency blocs might be organized. A split with the United States over the official price of gold might yet provoke the formation of a European bloc, although the June 11, 1974, agreement among the ten major industrial countries to use gold as collateral for international borrowing has averted that danger for the immediate future. European nations that face difficulties in paying for oil imports can now finance these payments, if necessary, by hocking their gold reserves. The United States has therefore agreed to share its largess—oil payments reinvested in New York by Arab producers—under specified conditions.

The United States will continue to oppose any uniform increase in the official price of gold. This opposition is based on the irrationality of using gold as the basis for the international monetary system and the preferability of substituting an internationally managed reserve base. The U.S. position may also be founded in part on a preference for continued use of the dollar as a reserve asset so long as neither special drawing rights (SDRs) issued by the IMF nor gold is able to force the dollar from its reserve asset role. In any event, the dollar is certain to continue in widespread international use as a transactions currency.

The United States and various European nations have sought to establish independent spheres of influence in the Southern Hemisphere. Initially, colonies or client states were sought as potential markets. Later, the governments of industrialized nations insisted on their right to intervene as protectors of investments made by private citizens in the Southern Hemisphere. Since the assertion of the Monroe Doctrine in 1823, the desire to minimize the influence of other Northern Hemisphere governments has been an important consideration prompting U.S. involvement in Latin America. Because political influence acquired by another government could potentially be used to the disadvantage of the United States, the latter felt an imperative need to maintain its hegemony. Although the United States has forsworn gunboat diplomacy (at least since U.S. intervention in the Dominican Republic), the government has hardly adopted a disinterested stance toward Latin America.

Germany and Italy lost their overseas territories as a consequence of World War I, and, following the Second World War, the United Kingdom bowed to demands for independence from most of its colonies. But France, while acceding to demands for independence, is seeking through economic and political ties to maintain a role in the African countries where it previously held sway.

Competition among the United States and the major European countries for influence in the Southern Hemisphere has been intensified by the growing scarcity of oil and other vital raw materials. The most direct clash is likely to be in the Middle East. During the first two decades following World War II, the United States government was content to let major American oil companies be the principal representatives of American influence and interests in the Arabian peninsula. By contrast, the Central Intelligence Agency (CIA) was prominent in Iran, and the State Department acted as the principal U.S. agent in Egypt. This distribution of responsibilities has been changing, and the State Department is assuming more and more direct control of U.S. relations in the Mideast. The major losers of influence will be American oil companies, since European governments are increasingly likely to negotiate agreements directly with the governments of producer states; and the U.S. government, if not an explicit party to contracts, will bear a growing direct responsibility to insure that American interests are protected and American influence expanded if possible.

The United States, Europe (with the exception of France), and Japan have agreed to a contingency plan for sharing available petroleum supplies in the event of another embargo. But in the absence of a similar crisis, the deterrent of high energy costs and the limited ability of consuming countries to finance payments deficits will govern the distribution of oil production among consumers. If, as expected, the United States proves to be a chief recipient of invested excess revenues earned by oil producers, it will bear a heavy responsibility for managing the recycling of these funds. To what extent and on what terms the U.S. government should intervene directly in capital markets to effect the recycling of oil-producer revenues is very much an open question. For example, if the United States relends these revenues to other industrial countries and the latter default, the United States will presumably be liable to the oil producers. How large a potential liability of this type do Americans want to assume? In the absence of U.S. efforts to bring about recycling, the multilateral pledges offered within the Organization for Economic Cooperation and Development (OECD) and the IMF not to engage in restrictions on payments for imports of goods or services would certainly be less credible.

Thus, particularly as an outgrowth of the difficulties created by the oil price increases, the United States is being obliged to assume the responsibility of distributing a largess and, possibly, also imposing sanctions. The motives for assuming this responsibility obviously include the desire to help maintain financial stability and high levels of real output throughout the industrial world. But U.S. efforts to prevent financial crises, depression, and trade restrictions have more than simply economic considerations behind them. The erosion of political ties between nations and the dangers of strident nationalism that could stem from these adverse developments are potent reasons for attempting to avoid economic reversals.

Canada

The United States and Canada are closely allied in the defense of North America, although the degree of influence Canada has in developing the strategy of this defense is probably minimal. In other respects, however, Canada has felt free to adopt an independent policy line, and differences between U.S. and Canadian approaches to the same issues have not led to serious friction. For example, Canada continued to trade with Cuba despite the U.S. embargo, Canada exported substantial volumes of wheat and smaller amounts of other products to mainland China when the United States still considered that nation an arch ideological foe, Canada remained aloof from the Vietnam War, and Canada has accepted American

men avoiding the draft as temporary residents and citizens. But differences between the United States and Canada in foreign policy have
not led to political differences preventing close military cooperation
in North America.

The issues that do contain the potential seeds of discord between
the United States and Canada are economic ones—specifically, U.S.
access to Canadian raw materials and American control of the
Canadian economy through the high level of U.S. investment in
that country. For example, in 1967, 45 percent of Canadian manufacturing industries were U.S.-controlled, as were 60 percent of the
petroleum and gas industry, and 56 percent of mining and smelting.
These percentages of U.S. control compare with 41 percent in manufacturing, 67 percent in petroleum and natural gas, and 49 percent
in mining and smelting in 1954. While the proportion of U.S. control
over the Canadian petroleum and natural gas industry declined over
this period, other foreign interests moved in, and the fraction of
Canadian control dropped from 31 to 26 percent.[4]

In response to this trend of growing U.S. control over critical
sectors of the Canadian economy, three studies were commissioned
by the Canadian government. The last of these investigations led to
legislation curtailing further American takeovers of Canadian firms
and the founding of the Canadian Development Corporation (CDC),
which is authorized to acquire foreign-controlled firms operating
in Canada. The most dramatic action of this type to date has been
the acquisition of Texas Gulf Sulfur by the CDC.

The critical long-term issue, related in part to the question of
U.S. domination of the Canadian economy, is the extent to which in
the future Canada will make available to the United States oil, gas,
lumber, hydroelectric power, and a variety of minerals. Canadians
can hardly be expected to impoverish themselves or to jeopardize
their own long-run economic development in order to fulfill the
scarce-resource needs of the United States. On the other hand, Canada
has suffered from high unemployment in recent years, and provincial
governments generally welcome U.S. investment as a means of reducing local unemployment and stimulating growth. Before the
1960s American investment was generally welcomed as a means of
supplementing inadequate domestic savings and of accelerating
growth. The recent competing desire to assert control over its own
economy will curtail to some degree Canada's reliance on the tech-

4 Foreign Direct Investment in Canada (Gray Report) (Ottawa: Government of
Canada, 1970), p. 20.

nical and financial wealth of the United States. But the extent of this shift, relative to the historical pattern, is uncertain. The change will most likely be gradual and modest.

Japan

The United States is committed to protect Japan under its nuclear umbrella and would presumably retaliate with nuclear weapons against any enemy that struck Japan. The extent of the American commitment to defend Japanese territory with U.S. troops is far less clear: there is no appreciable U.S. troop concentration in Japan, Okinawa has reverted to the Japanese, and the Japanese have their own self-defense forces to repel invaders.

No serious political differences exist between the United States and Japan. Both countries are committed to democracy and to the capitalistic exploitation of economic opportunity within the limitations set by their own respective societies. In the United States the constraint is an antitrust law that is both out-of-date and enforced primarily against smaller monopolies. In Japan the constraint is to observe domestically the mores of the government-business family. This standard allows wider discretion for Japanese externally than at home.

Potential conflicts between the United States and Japan arise from the fact that there is a high degree of mutual interdependence between the economies of the two nations and, at the same time, the two are competing for scarce supplies of raw materials throughout the world. The United States is Japan's single largest export customer, and Japan is a major purchaser in the United States of soybeans, grain, lumber, aircraft, computers, and a variety of highly sophisticated manufactured goods. The Japanese may also be a major user of U.S.-mined coal in coming years.

Although conflicts will certainly arise between the United States and Japan over a variety of economic issues, the overriding common interests of the two nations will probably force compromises leading to the resolution of differences. The short-lived American embargo on exports of soybeans and protein feed substitutes in the summer of 1973 struck most directly at Japan. The validity of Japanese concerns, the strength of their reaction, and the possible losses to American farmers from new drives for agricultural self-sufficiency in Japan (and Europe) have impressed the lesson on American policymakers.

There is probably more reluctance now on the part of U.S. officials to use export controls as a domestic anti-inflationary device than there was before the experiences of last year.

Differences over trade in textiles have apparently been resolved by a new Arrangement Regarding International Trade in Textiles, which became effective on January 1, 1974. This comprehensive agreement includes all major fibers and producers, with explicit protection for smaller suppliers. Global overcapacity in the steel industry, which a few years ago provoked a clash between Americans and the Japanese, has now also disappeared. In international monetary affairs, the Japanese seem willing either to accept any reasonable consensus position or to float the yen independently if this alternative seems expedient.

Oil producers have recognized that Japanese purchasers are generally willing to pay higher prices than buyers from other industrial countries are willing to pay. This circumstance does not necessarily work to the detriment of the United States, since the demands of the most avaricious producers can be satisfied and Americans and purchasers from other nations can then enter the market and obtain oil at a somewhat lower cost.

Although economic issues are likely to present the most contentious set of problems between the two countries, neither the United States nor Japan can afford any major disagreement.

The Soviet Union

Between the United States and the Soviet Union there exists an uneasy military balance based on an approximate parity in strength and horror of the consequences should either party be moved to employ a significant fraction of its ultimate destructive capability. Tension between the two countries stems not only from competition for territorial control and influence, but also from contending political ideologies. Fortunately, both countries are run by bureaucracies that dull the cutting edge of their respective ideological orientations and appreciate their common interests.

But this area of common interest makes European states and many developing countries worry that the United States and the Soviet Union may ultimately agree on an implicit partitioning of the world. In that event, each of the major powers would abstain from interfering within the other's sphere of influence and would be free to exercise ultimate sway within its own area. Any such arrangement between the United States and the Soviet Union could have obvious unfortunate consequences for the smaller fish in each pond.

American policy toward the Soviet Union is the clearest example we have today of the use of economic concessions by the United States to obtain military security and political benefits. The Soviet Union has far more to gain from expanded trade and technological transfers between the two countries than does the United States. This circumstance is apparently well understood by Senator Jackson, Representative Vanik, and supporters of the position that political, in addition to economic, concessions should be obtained from the Soviet Union if that nation is to be granted most favored nation (MFN) tariff status and access to Export-Import Bank financing. The opening of trade with the Soviet Union on an MFN basis clearly does not include an equitable quid pro quo for the United States if the arrangement is restricted to economic transactions exclusively.

What then is the outlook for relations between the United States and the Soviet Union as influenced by economic considerations? Increased economic contact will help to reduce tension and present the opportunity for greater numbers of individual Americans and Russians to become acquainted with one another as people. These personal interrelationships are one of the greatest benefits of international commerce and investment.

But grounds for competition will persist, and tension will remain. Probably one of the most serious factors leading to difficulties will be the inequality of benefits accuring to the United States and the Soviet Union from an increase in economic contact between the two. Thus, demands for political concessions from the Soviets are likely to be appended to legislation granting the president authority to remove barriers to trade, investment, and technological transfers. Such conditions will undoubtedly be resented by the Soviets, who may claim that political issues are not relevant to increased economic intercourse. On the other hand, neither party will be able to turn away from the other, since both are vitally interested in reducing tension.

China

Given the continuing gradual disengagement of the United States from Indochina, if not the total termination of hostilities there, no military confrontation between the United States and China is foreseeable. Presumably the status of Taiwan will remain in limbo; the mainland Chinese will not attempt to take over the island, nor will an invasion be launched against the mainland.

In current U.S. relations with China economic contact is being used to bridge political differences, and, as is the case with the Soviet Union, the Chinese potentially have much more to gain economically from this interchange than does the United States. But since there are no major political concessions that Americans choose to obtain from the Chinese, the same sources of tension and disagreement do not exist. Even more than is the case with Japan, the mechanics of U.S. foreign policy with China are almost entirely economic.

Economic contact between Americans and the Chinese will continue to increase, subject to the aversion of the Chinese to large payments deficits with the United States. Commerce with China will be a barely noticeable contribution to the total volume of U.S. exports and imports. But since the United States will probably continue, after Japan, to be China's second most important trading partner, the relationship will be important to the Chinese and therefore significant to Americans as a means for increasing communication and strengthening political ties.

Developing Countries

Most of the issues between the United States and developing nations are economic ones relating to the utilization of resources—including labor—or the sharing of the fruits from such utilization. By contrast, threats to territorial security and tensions arising from differences of political ideology are minimal. No developing country can physically threaten the United States, and the United States has forsworn the use of gunboat diplomacy. Nevertheless, the United States and American corporations are not above employing underhanded tactics to advance or protect what are considered to be vital interests. In most cases political ideology seems unimportant, since policymakers have learned to tolerate almost any type of foreign political regime that is sufficiently friendly toward U.S. economic interests.

The list of economic issues arising between the United States and developing countries still includes the traditional ones of the extent and terms of financial assistance for development and the effects of American investment on the economies of developing countries. More recent questions focus on access of growing foreign manufacturing industries to the markets of the United States and American access to oil and other raw materials produced abroad. As revenues from the production of oil accumulate, Americans will be forced to review the pros and cons of foreign direct investment here. If foreign countries do grant the United States access to their supplies of oil and other minerals, the United States will be expected to reciprocate in terms of the access it grants foreigners to agricultural products and other basic commodities produced in the United States. Finally, there is the question of the resources that historically have been assumed to be available to all countries but the property of none, namely, the resources found on and under the deeper portions of the seabed.

In attempting to evaluate the future impact of economic issues on U.S. foreign policy toward developing countries, it is useful to divide the list of issues into two groups: those that give the poorer nations a bargaining lever to be used against the United States, and those that, conversely, grant the United States the ability to demand concessions from developing countries. Among the first group of issues—those giving nonaffluent countries some ability to influence U.S. policy—are the following: access to oil and other raw materials, the choice of investing revenues derived from the sale of oil in the United States or in other industrial countries, and the terms under which U.S. direct investment enterprises will be permitted to operate abroad or, in confrontations, the type and amount of compensation given for the expropriation of such enterprises. Issues conferring bargaining strength upon the United States in its dealings with developing countries are these: the amount and terms of financial assistance for economic development, the degree of access to U.S. markets for imported manufactured goods, the availability of U.S. agricultural products and other basic materials (including the amount of food aid for famine relief), and the extent to which the United States, as a policy decision, concedes a share in the profits from the exploitation of the ocean floor to poor countries.

The preceding categorization suggests that countries with low average personal disposable incomes but rich in natural resources hold most of the developing world's bargaining chips in confrontations with the United States. By contrast, the threats the United States can wield are particularly effective against developing countries that are not particularly well endowed with natural resources. This absence of direct comparability between conceivable threats and possible concessions may lead to a sense of frustration on the part of

Americans, particularly those who do not possess detailed knowledge of the issues and the characteristics of various developing countries. The same mismatching of weapons and vulnerabilities is likely to produce tensions between resource-rich and resource-poor developing nations. Since the oil producers will most likely either not be inclined or not possess the administrative capablity to fully compensate oil-poor developing countries for the adverse impact of the increase in petroleum prices, a serious economic injury will be added to existing religious and cultural differences. Relations between the two groups of developing countries are therefore likely to be awkward indeed.

How will the United States operate in this environment? The only meaningful offer the United States can make to producers of oil and other minerals is access to its markets through imports or foreign investment in the United States. One of the most common reasons for direct investment abroad offered by U.S. multinational corporations is their avowed inability to retain or expand their share of a foreign market without establishing, at first, distributional and service networks abroad. Overseas manufacturing operations, producing goods tailored to local requirements and tastes, usually follow. The oil producers, as they use their revenues to finance industrialization, may well desire to follow the same pattern. Other developing nations that are now beginning to industrialize, such as Brazil, Mexico, Taiwan, and Korea, will also want access to U.S. markets.

The offer of unrestricted access to U.S. markets for manufactured consumer goods is more carrot than stick. The United States in fact does not possess an effective stick to be used against producers of oil or other scarce minerals. The oil producers will have an abundance of revenues, and acceptable if slightly inferior substitutes for any service or product the United States might deny oil producers can be purchased elsewhere. Because the success of U.S. policies in dealing with the resource-rich nations of the Southern Hemisphere will depend so much on persuasion rather than coercion, the example this country sets toward all developing countries is critical.

Two issues are especially important in establishing the U.S. example. First, what kind of access will the United States give foreigners to agricultural commodities, timber, coal, and other basic resources produced in the United States? Second, what position will the United States adopt toward sharing the benefits from exploiting resources on and below the seabed?

Of all the products in short supply in the United States, and therefore subject to larger than average price increases, agricultural commodities are the most sensitive. Basically, either of two kinds of policies can be adopted regarding sales of scarce agricultural commodities to foreigners. The government can resolve not to intervene in the market but to permit Americans and foreigners to compete for available supplies on a precisely equal footing, that is, purchase whatever amounts they desire at whatever prices result from the untrammeled play of supply and demand. Or the government can decide to allocate supplies of commodities deemed scarce according to a predetermined set of priorities. The most likely list of priorities would place the American consumer first, foreign countries stricken by famine second, regular foreign purchasers third, and all other foreigners last. The adoption of an allocation system based on priorities is the more likely alternative.

What the reaction in developing countries would be to this type of allocation program is not entirely clear. While the U.S. responsibility, as largest single food producer in the world, to aid countries suffering from famine would be explicitly recognized, the American consumer would still be first on the list of priorities, and Americans probably waste more food per capita than do citizens of any other country. If the priority schedule were further refined to allow for the sale of a specified quantity of grain and oilseeds to low-income nations at concessional prices, the overseas reaction would be positive. Such a scheme would probably satisfy demands for government intervention to help curb the rising cost of food in the United States, and its external features would be commendable on equity grounds. In addition, adoption of this plan—which apparently is embodied only partially in legislation under consideration—would give the United States a strong argument for insisting that oil producers also make their product available to resource-poor developing countries on concessional terms.

Given prospective shortages of critical minerals and the technological capability of the United States, exceeding that of any other country, to exploit the resources of the seabed, some Americans may advocate the position that in the deeper part of the sea, beyond the continental shelf or beyond a 200-mile limit, a nation and its entrepreneurs should be entitled to the full rewards of whatever riches they are able to obtain. Developing countries would, of course, find any such stance avaricious. In fact, the U.S. position apparently will be to acknowledge at least a partial international claim to deep-sea resources and to offer royalty payments to an agency that would use these funds to benefit the world's poor.

The old chestnuts of U.S. foreign economic relations with developing countries are the impact of American direct investment abroad and the amount of American financial contribution to development assistance. These issues have been linked by the United States, in that American representatives have opposed World Bank and Interamerican Development Bank loans to countries that had expropriated U.S. firms and had not paid adequate compensation and were not actively negotiating such payment.

American-owned firms in developing countries maintain that they bring a variety of benefits in the form of increased employment; the introduction of modern technology, training and experience for production workers and managers drawn from the local population; and a general stimulus to economic growth through the economies of scale resulting from expansion of the domestic market. Critics of investment in developing countries by major corporations point to inadequate wages, low royalties for the extraction of minerals, the establisment of an industrial sector that has minimal contact with the more backward portions of the domestic economy, resistance to local participation through either the sale of equity or the training of nationals as managers, the encouragement of wasteful habits of consumption patterned after those in the United States, and intervention in the politics of host countries. The net balance of the costs and benefits resulting from U.S. investment in developing countries is relevant to U.S. foreign policy. The varying estimates of this net outcome, calculated either explicitly or implicitly by foreign policymakers, will largely determine the type of demands and restrictions that foreign governments will place on U.S. firms investing abroad. How the U.S. government defends what it interprets as the rights and privileges of U.S. firms overseas will depend in part on the similar estimates of American officials regarding the effects of investment abroad.

Because of the absence of a security threat from developing countries and the indifference on the part of U.S. officials regarding whether these nations exist under democratic or totalitarian governments, American foreign policy toward the resource-poor nations of the Southern Hemisphere tends to be much more a business-oriented policy than it is in other areas of the world.

Although the activities of many U.S. business firms operating in developing countries are still characterized by exploitational practices, attitudes and perceptions have changed from the days of banana republics and gunboat diplomacy, when business at home and abroad was invariably good for the United States and the inhabitants of poor nations were to be happy with whatever they got. Today the U.S. government accepts the right of other governments to expropriate U.S. firms, and the executives of U.S. corporations operating overseas recognize that their firms have economic and social responsibilities to their host countries. The major impact of U.S. foreign policy on developing countries probably does not grow out of confrontational situations, but out of the daily decisions and advice from State and Commerce Department personnel that help establish the environment in which U.S. investors operate.

In addition to the interplay described above between major American firms, the U.S. government, and foreign governments, business interests have occasionally forced the U.S. government to adopt positions on issues that officials might otherwise have preferred to ignore or let slide. For example, the profitable opportunities for trade with Cuba and the possibility of partial restitution for properties seized constitute a significant reason for considering a change in the U.S. official stance toward that country.[5] American commerce with Rhodesia raised another set of awkward issues for the State Department.

The extent of financial assistance for economic development granted in former years has been determined primarily by the interaction of the pleas of humanitarians, the cajoling of lobbyists representing export interests, and the bitching of taxpayers. The outcome of this contention has been a steady decline in the amount of bilateral funding provided. The increase in oil prices, despite subsequent congressional approval of a refinancing package for the International Development Association, also raises the possibility of future objections to multilateral development financing if the Arab oil producers do not partially offset the adverse impact of increased prices on the balance-of-payments positions and the development plans of resource-poor, low-income countries.

[5] In addition, a staff report prepared for the use of the Senate Committee on Foreign Relations says: "It is my conclusion that the Cubans are correct when they say, as one did, that the U.S. policy of isolating Cuba has been a failure. If this is so, then it follows a new policy should be devised." The statutory means for reexamining and changing current policies are then discussed. U.S., Congress, Senate, Report by Pat M. Holt for the Committee on Foreign Relations, 93d Cong., 2d sess., 1974, p. 11.

Conclusion

The foregoing review of the diverse foreign policy goals of the United States and the interplay of actions designed to achieve these various goals suggests that in the next decade economic considerations will have a more significant impact on the formulation of U.S. foreign policy than was the case in the 1950s or 1960s. This conclusion could be overturned by the appearance of a major threat to the territorial security of the United States, but at present such an eventuality seems unlikely. Even in the most volatile area of the world today—the Mideast—U.S. foreign policy is strongly colored by economic considerations.

Among the economic issues that are likely to receive most attention, access to basic commodities and raw materials will probably be outstanding. This issue will affect U.S. relations with Europe, Canada, Japan, and the developing countries. In addition, troop costs and the existence of tariff and nontariff trade barriers will have a major impact on relations with Europe. During periods of strong international inflationary pressures, Japan will remain concerned about the possibility of U.S.-imposed controls on exports of grain, soybeans, lumber, scrap metals, and possibly other commodities. The extent of U.S. investment abroad and the activities of American firms operating in other countries will continue to be of particular significance in Canada and the less developed world. On the other hand, as the revenues of the oil producers accumulate, the extent and type of long-term foreign investment in the United States will grow in importance as an issue.

Trade and a limited volume of investment will be utilized as vehicles for improving political relations with the Soviet Union and China. But because the economic exchange will be unbalanced, and because there are political concessions the United States would like to win from the Soviet Union, economic relations with that country particularly will be troubled by demands for policy changes on the part of the Soviet government.

The amount and type of assistance given to promote economic development will continue to be an issue between the United States and poor nations. As these countries industrialize, they will demand, and most likely get, improved access to U.S. markets for manufactured goods.

To return to a question posed above, during the next decade or two, will economic considerations substantially determine who are the military allies and opponents of the United States and the degree of support the U.S. government will lend to other governments, whether democratic, authoritarian, or whatever? Economic considerations cannot be expected to produce a major reshuffling of allies and antagonists. The United States will still be allied primarily with Canada, Japan, and Western Europe, and will still contend primarily with the Soviet Union. Long-standing ideological and cultural orientations cannot be wiped away quickly.

However, economic factors will influence more heavily in the future than during the decades since World War II the tenor of U.S. foreign policy. Economic common interests will ease old hostilities, and new economic conflicts are likely to intensify existing antagonisms and possibly create new enemies. But especially within each of the three major groups of countries—the industrialized Western societies (including Japan), the socialized countries of Eastern Europe and Asia, and the Southern Hemisphere—economic considerations will heavily influence which individual countries are considered to be the friends of the United States and which are the antagonists.

Soviet Commercial Relations and Political Change

John P. Hardt

SOVIET leaders, especially Leonid Brezhnev, appear to perceive an urgent need for improvement in economic performance. Increased economic growth through modernization of the civilian economy and improved consumer incentives are the central features of the plan for change set out in the Ninth Five-Year Plan. Commercial relations with the West, including the United States, centering on transfer of technology, appear to constitute the preferred route for enhancing the growth and quality of economic output.

In the West it is hoped that Soviet economic problems may lead to a diversion of resources from military programs and to reform of economic mechanisms, which might, in turn, reinforce this economic shift away from the arms race. The central question of this essay is: Will high-technology Soviet commercial relations with the industrial West—especially the United States—reduce or enhance the likelihood of change in resource allocation policy and economic reform? The rationale developed herein is that in the interest of maximum economic performance the prospects of change in resource allocation policy and reform will be enhanced. Commercial relations alone will not be enough. More resources for providing an adequate infrastructure from domestic programs and selective reform in those areas of priority foreign-technology transfer would greatly enhance the effectiveness of the commercial-technology bridge. To be sure, the political cost of reducing the share of economic increments to the military and facilitating professionalizaton of the economic processes that have long been within the control of the Party *apparatchiki* would be high. But, assuming the economic benefits added by these changes would be significant and considered vital to the top leadership, the changes are likely, in time.

Many contributed to this essay: among them, Lawrence Brainard, Warren Eason, Murray Feshbach, Gregory Grossman, George Holliday, Kent Hughes, Franklyn Holzman, Theodore Shabad, and John R. Thomas. Responsibility for the content remains that of the author.

Diversion of resources from incremental military to new civilian programs is especially likely if new and serious economic crises arise and security opportunities or risks do not become dominant. An extremely bad weather year for construction and agriculture, in the absence of any opportunity to demonstrate military superiority or any threat to Soviet territorial integrity, might be the catalytic condition for change. This is not a prediction but an identification of a putative rationale for a course of change.

Moreover, with no change in resource allocation policy and/or selective economic reform, commercial relations are not likely to have the beneficial effects desired by the leadership. More cars and trucks without more roads, repair services, and a better-managed transport system are likely to leave the Soviet economy worse off than before. So the transfer of Western technology via trade may be for the Soviets more a means of digging themselves deeper into their economic problem areas than an escape mechanism or a means to bail themselves out painlessly.

The Interplay of Trade, Economic Priorities, and Reform

Concurrent with the summit agreement, there has been an upsurge in commercial relations between the Soviet Union and the United States. Trade turnover increased from $.2 to $1.4 billion in the period 1971–73 (1973: U.S. exports, $1.2 billion; imports, $.2 billion).[1] The United States may become the principal trading partner of the Soviet Union among the economically developed nations. Paralleling the increased Soviet reliance on Western economic sources was the formulation of Soviet economic policy as manifested in the Ninth Five-Year Plan (1971–75), highlighting technological change and im-

---

[1] U.S., Dept. of Commerce, Bureau of East-West Trade, *Bulletin*, Feb. 7, 1974. For more detailed discussion of these problems, see U.S., Congress, House, Report by John Hardt and George Holliday to the Committee on Foreign Affairs, *U.S.-Soviet Commercial Relations: The Interplay of Economics, Technology Transfer, and Diplomacy*, 93d Cong., 1st sess., 1973, pp. 45 ff. (hereafter *U.S.-Soviet Commercial Relations*); U.S., Congress, Joint Economic Committee, *Soviet Economic Prospects for the Seventies*, 93d Cong., 1st sess., 1973 (hereafter *Soviet Economic Prospects for the Seventies*); U.S., Congress, Joint Economic Committee, Hearings, *Soviet Economic Outlook*, 93d Cong., 1st sess., July 1973 (hereafter *Soviet Economic Outlook*); Norton T. Dodge, ed., *Summit: A Year Later*, Symposium of the Washington Chapter of the AAASS, May 1973 (Mechanicsville, Md.: Cremona Press, 1973), contributions by Robert Kovach, James Noren, and John Hardt.

provement in the lot of the consumer.[2] The availability of Western—
especially American—technology is to play a critical role in attempts
to fulfill this plan, possibly even acting as a bottleneck.

The Soviet Union has now begun to move into the international
economic system of markets and finances. Leonid Brezhnev has per-
sonally proclaimed the end of the Stalinist policy of autarky, or
self-sufficiency;[3] and the acceptability of trade with the advanced
industrial nations, first approved by Nikita Khrushchev in the late
1950s, has taken a major step forward. Especially important is the
commercial joining of the economic fortunes of the United States
and the Soviet Union—the long-time adversaries of the cold war.

The new political climate fostering trade has been the permissive
context within which the urgent needs of the Soviet economy for
advanced industrial and agricultural processes have generated a
long and expanding shopping list for Soviet purchases—especially in
the U.S. market. Energy extraction and processing equipment, mass-
production equipment such as foundries for truck production, computers and related systems, agribusiness processes and agricultural
products—all are high on Soviet lists. The new economic policy of
selective reliance on Western sources for high-technology products
may not be enough. Without a shift of Soviet resource policy from
the high-priority programs of the past military, heavy industry, and
space and significant changes in the Soviet system of planning and
management, this expensive-technology bridge may provide results
far short of both planned and potential achievements. On the other
hand, the political cost of maximizing the economic benefit of
technological transfers may be too great. However, pressure may build
over time to significantly revise the economic institutions and to shift
the military-dominated resource prorities in order to gain some
return on this commercial opening to the West.

Western technology has been in vogue before, not only in the
Soviet period but during tsarist rule. Why change now, when the
economic system has seemingly stood the test of time? And if changes
are to occur, why not temporary Western technological borrowing
insulated from the domestic system of rule?

The Stalinist economic policy was built on three pillars: (1) a con-

---

2 N. K. Baibakov, *Gosudarstvennyi pyatiletnyi plan razvitiia narodnogo khoziaistva SSSR na 1971–1975 gody* [State Five-Year Plan for development of the
U.S.S.R. national economy for the period 1971–1975] (Moscow: Politizdat, Apr.
1972).

3 Brezhnev, speech on West German television, *Pravda*, May 22, 1973.

centration of resources on programs designed to broaden the heavy industrial and defense production base of the economy, i.e., *the priority system for resource allocation*; (2) an institutional system of control designed to organize and channel the productive energies of the economy into priority sectors with minimum reliance on the type of material incentives usually associated with the market process, i.e., *the control or command system of planning and management*; and (3) independence from foreign sources of goods and services, the policy of self-sufficiency or nonforeign reliance, i.e., *the policy of foreign trade autarky*.

The Stalinist economic policy of the 1930s correlated a foreign policy of isolation and hostility with a domestic policy of ever tightening control and orthodoxy. To be sure, foreign sources of technology were important to Stalin in establishing the industrial base. But once a minimum level of technology was attained in fields such as machine-building, metal processing, and energy output, foreign influences were purged and commercial relations reduced by design to an absolute minimum. Independence from foreign commercial relations had its benefits, as the export prices of raw materials—grain, timber, oil, furs—were at a low point in the world market, especially as compared with industrial imports. This phenomenon led in the 1930s to the so-called foreign trade scissors crisis. The export price of Soviet raw materials such as grain and oil fell drastically as compared with the import prices of Western industrial equipment—the price trends thus being comparable to an open scissors.[4] Moreover, during the world depression, technology was not dynamic, and transfers of foreign technology could be suspended for some years without bringing about a technology lag.

The opening to the West under Stalin via imports of Western technology and specialists into the Soviet Union in the late 1920s and early 1930s has been likened to the periodic waves of Russian interest in Western means for updating Russian society associated in earlier times with Peter the Great, Catherine, and Count Witte in the reign of the last tsar. The special Soviet-Western relationship during World War II, when the Soviet Union obtained from the West both the military and the economic sinew for its defense against Nazi Germany, is sometimes added to this cyclic pattern. In each of these previous openings to the West, the commercial rela-

[4] For a discussion of the foreign trade "scissors crisis" of 1930 and 1931, see Maurice Dobb, *Soviet Economic Development since 1917* (New York: International Publishers, 1948), p. 238.

tionships were temporary; priorities were primarily military-oriented; the domestic regime was, if anything, more authoritarian than the present one; and reduction in hostility toward Western countries was, at best, short-run.

Will this most recent opening of Soviet Russia to the West be different? Perhaps yes. There are expectations for significant Soviet internal change relating to this opening. Specifically, there is some expectation of the following: (1) a long-term, expanding commercial relationship between the Soviet Union and Western advanced industrial nations, especially involving continued, perhaps expanding, transfers of technology; (2) a reordering of Soviet priorities, holding constant or reducing defense-related activities in order to increase growth-related programs that may be expected to maximize the economic modernization facilitated by the technology transfer; (3) a reasonably irreversible reform or modernization of the Soviet process of planning and management to provide an institutional framework for improved economic efficiency.

Serious reservations concerning all of these expectations are evident, and they may be summarized in the following manner. Even though Brezhnev has announced an end to the policy of economic isolation, he probably does not wish to become dependent on Western, especially American, products and technology over the long term. The use of trade leverage to influence Soviet emigration policy has demonstrated to him the dangers of such dependence, if he was not already fully aware of them. Moreover, significant changes in priorities can only be brought about by shifts away from new military resource claimants and to civilian ones. Strong Party resistance to such shifts will doubtless continue to be evident. Finally, professionalization and decentralization of economic planning and management can only be brought about by a revision, perhaps a diminution, in the Party's control of Soviet society. It is therefore credibly argued that General Secretary Brezhnev will prefer to minimize the effects of internal and external policy changes required to modernize the Soviet economy and revive its growth rate.

Modernization of Soviet society and stimulation of lagging economic performance are not in dispute in the Soviet Union. But the acceptable means to attain these objectives are open to question. Three views may be suggested as having some currency in the Soviet leadership group. For shorthand purposes we may refer to these as: the costless approach; the collapse theory approach; and the flexible, pragmatic approach. To be sure, the first two are partially extremes designed to establish parameters for discussing the range of possibilities under the third variant. However there appear to be adherents to each view. (Soviet leaders, of course, do not use the descriptive titles we have chosen to label these views.)

The Costless Approach

If it were possible to meet the plans for technological and economic improvement within the current institutional framework and without a major reordering of priorities, the best of all possible worlds would be attained, from the standpoint of the Soviet leadership, and a politically and ideologically costless solution would be possible. This approach would be even more attractive if expanding commercial relations with the United States for critical bottleneck technology transfers to the Soviet economy were to be financed by a combination of long-term, low-interest credits, and if repayment could be made solely via foreign extraction of unexploited raw material sources. This insulated and self-liquidating commercial tie to the West would seem to be a politically, ideologically, and economically costless approach to economic improvement in the Soviet Union. Moreover, Soviet missile, naval, and ground forces might continue to expand at the rate of the 1960s to attain a possible goal of superiority not only in Eurasia but in the world. Brezhnev is said to have voiced a version of this view to East European leaders after the Washington summit in June 1973.[5]

The Collapse Theory Approach

Presumably there are those among the Soviet leadership who agree with Stalin's view that an end of economic isolation will lead to an opening of the Soviet system to subversive foreign influences. If an effective program for reviving economic growth via foreign technology necessarily meant subverting the Soviet system to one reflecting economic priorities closer to those of a comparatively disarmed Japan and the mixed private government system of a market-oriented U.S. economy, then the Marxist-Leninist system of the Soviet state would be the price paid for change. This convergence of the Soviet system with those of the industrial West would imply the political and ideological collapse of Lenin's and Stalin's system of priorities and control, and would certainly be unacceptable to all

5 *New York Times*, Sept. 17, 1973.

of the Soviet leadership. We are not privy to the inner councils of the Politburo, but some of the more ideologically rigid opponents of Brezhnev's policy of détente may have argued the collapse or subversion theory. Put another way, this seems to be the kind of view Brezhnev's spokesmen were arguing against, the view of the so-called other people in Soviet leading circles.

The Flexible, Pragmatic Approach

It may be that neither the hopes of the first nor the fears of the second school in Soviet leadership have been borne out, and that a more flexible, pragmatic view is emerging. It is unlikely that the Soviet leaders would continue to adhere to the costless approach. It may be increasingly unrealistic and unfeasible to assume costless transfer of foreign technology to the Soviet economy. It may also be politically unlikely to expect preferential credit and price treatment in the current state of American–Soviet commercial relations. To move toward a more flexible variant may be economically desirable and politically acceptable.

This is not to imply that the optimal position, preferable to either of the two extremes, would be on a convergence path. Although the political costs might be maximal in convergence, the economic gains might be diminishing. Likewise, there might be some political gains in a shift away from the traditional operation of the current, modified Stalinist system. It is often suggested that modernization and professionalism are in necessary conflict with Leninist precepts of Party control. The inability of the system to accommodate dissidents such as Aleksandr Solzhenitsyn and Andrei Sakharov is said to be illustrative of this dilemma. However, this may be too mechanical a view. There may be a reason for distinguishing between the Leninist and Stalinist systems, as some East Europeans have chosen to do.[6] The Stalinist system may have been rigidly unique to the issues of its stage of development, involving the transition from a rural to an urban-industrial economy and the establishment of a modern military base. It perhaps also reflected the personality of its architect and master—Joseph Stalin. With the attainment of military power and industrialization, and the death of Stalin, the imperatives of change may now become compelling toward modernization within a more flexible Leninist system. Andrei Sakharov may have been

6 Czech reformers such as Joseph Goldman, for example, argued that the Stalinist system is no longer appropriate.

more correct in his earlier program, calling for a "second economic revolution" within the Soviet system, than in a later paper in which he seems to conclude that elimination of the Soviet system is Russia's only salvation.[7] He may also be wrong in thinking that a democratic, Western type of market system would be optimal for the Soviet Union.[8] The cost-benefit optimal may not be in system convergence but in a new socialist-Leninist market-simulating system. The increasing high-technology transfer inherent in expanding commercial relations may increase the likelihood of a shift in priorities and changes in Soviet economic institutions away from a Stalinist to a less rigid, less authoritarian Leninist system. Without such changes, the Soviet Union is likely to receive less than optimal economic results from foreign-technology transfer. Pressure for change is likely to arise in the specific areas singled out in the current plans for priorities—raw material extraction and processing, mass-production industrial processes, computer-assisted systems, and agribusiness. Each of these areas will be assessed in terms of the gains to Soviet economic performance from foreign-technology transfer through the interaction of expanded commercial relations, reordering priorities, and economic reform. We acknowledge that the logic of this interactive approach might appear to provide maximum economic benefits and, at the same time, maximum political costs. So it is not surprising that attempts are being made in many cases to reduce the political cost of change in institutions and priorities without adversely affecting the economic gain from technology transfers. This appears to be difficult. Thus, compromises are likely, at least in the short run, with an initial approach as close as possible to the "costless approach." However, in the long run, although importation of high-technology products alone may fill critical bottlenecks in supply plans, these products may not have a significant multiplier effect on Soviet output.

Franklyn Holzman has discussed the negative multiplier, that is, "the sequential process by which an autonomous interruption of imported intermediate products will disrupt output." He argues that bottlenecks interrupting trade are more damaging to output expectations in a planned economy, with a specified and unchangeable bill of goods, than they are in a market economy, where bills of goods

7 "Appeal of Scientists A. D. Sakharov, V. F. Turchin and R. A. Medvedev to Soviet Party and Government Leaders" (Mar. 19, 1970), *Survey*, Summer 1970, pp. 160–70.

8 Sakharov to Brezhnev, *New York Times*, Aug. 18, 1972.

may be more readily changed.[9] We would consider the multiplier effect on production, from coupling the investment derived from imported high-technology products with additional Soviet domestic investment and reform in planning and management, to maximize the sequential, incremental effect on production. For example, the importation of U.S. feeder lots for expanding Soviet animal husbandry may have a certain positive incremental effect on meat output. However, if, by additional Soviet infrastructure investment and reorganization of the administration of Soviet animal husbandry, the much higher U.S. level of productivity might be attained, the increase would be several times the beneficial effect from using the imported technology alone. In general, the multiplier effect of technological imports would probably be markedly higher if high quality Soviet investment resources were shifted from other Soviet domestic programs, especially military programs, in order to supply an integrated production supply and distribution infrastructure.

The need for efficiency in planning and management further dictates changes, both in specific enterprise areas and at the national level, in order to fully exploit the economic potential of the new programs. Since such reforms require downgrading the resource claims of very powerful bureaucracies and changes in the economic control system of the Party, second- or third-best economic solutions may be tried first and may persist. However, second- or third-best economic solutions are not preordained if they can be demonstrated to be operational within Soviet countervailing political positions. The improvement in factor efficiency from increased energy output, better planning, and improved material incentives provided by automobiles and meat is not institutionally inconsistent with either the Soviet principles of the nation's Leninist past or the experience of Western industrial nations whose productivity the Soviet leaders wish to emulate. The problem, then, is to emulate best Western factor proportions and technology without adopting characteristics of market economies that too sharply threaten the political control system and priorities of the Party. This is a practical question for traditional claimants of power and resources: What political costs are worth paying for improved economic efficiency? It is also an ideological question for the Party hierarchy: How flexible is Leninism? However, it is worth noting that the political and ideological costs may not be viewed uniformly within the Party hierarchy and entrenched

9 "Import Bottlenecks and the Foreign Trade Multiplier," *Western Economic Journal*, June 1969, pp. 101–8.

bureaucracies. The summit of Soviet power may be least adversely affected and benefit most from change. So Brezhnev may act differently in implementing his program of commercial opening to the West than his Soviet *apparatchiki* or tsarist predecessors. Still, Brezhnev must also remember that this same Party bureaucracy first kept Nikita Khrushchev in power and then probably assisted in his removal to make way for the present leadership.

Bottlenecks in Plan Fulfillment

The principal Soviet import requirements from the West, especially from the United States, are representative of the critical bottlenecks in fulfilling Soviet plans. Moreover, the impact on output of increased foreign imports will be significantly greater if more resources are shifted from other priority projects—often those related to military supply—and more modern and efficient methods of planning and management are adopted. In most cases this choice is not likely to represent the current Soviet approach. Quite the contrary, it appears that while importation of technology is being pushed, a minimal shift in priorities, especially from military programs, and moderate reforms are the rule rather than the exception. However, these efforts to insulate the changes in foreign trade from domestic priorities, planning, and management may not only minimize the potential benefits of imports but actually reduce to ineffectiveness the whole program of technological transfer. Whether the Soviet leadership recognizes or would accept the cost in institutional change, diminution of Party control, and weakening of some entrenched bureaucracies in order to improve economic performance is an open question. Let us examine the hypothesis that they would, in the context of several important examples: (1) petroleum and natural gas extraction, processing, and transmission; (2) computer-related systems in planning and management; (3) mass industrial production processes, such as those of the automotive industry; and (4) agribusiness activities, such as animal husbandry. In each of these activities it appears that significant importation from the West, especially the United States, is planned, but that domestic enterprise plans and management appear to be largely modifications of the traditionalist centralized command economy. While the full resource requirements for domestic investment may be far less than currently projected, the investment share in each case appears to be rising.

These four economic sectors appear to be critical in the Soviet view toward improving the productivity of capital and labor. Without significant improvement in factor efficiency and reduction in the defense priority, Soviet growth is likely to fall short of plan in 1971–75 (the Ninth Five-Year Plan) and 1976–80 (the Tenth Five-Year Plan). Based on projections of past factor productivity, the projected growth rate will do well to average 4 percent in GNP per annum.[10] Current Soviet plan fulfillment projections for the Ninth Five–Year Plan would place the required rate closer to 6 percent.[11] In 1972 the growth rate was about 2 percent. While the growth rate in 1973 probably exceeded the 6-percent figure, the shortfalls in the early years of the plan were not recouped.[12] Soviet leaders and planners may not yet think primarily in these aggregative terms, but the specific economic activities enumerated below are perhaps more illustrative of their concepts of plan fulfillment: (1) more energy, primarily from hydrocarbons, i.e., oil and natural gas; (2) a better information system and research-planning-management system based on advanced computer applications; (3) improved transporation for goods and people through the output of more trucks and cars; (4) a visible and qualitative improvement in the diet via expanded meat output.

In the Soviet Ninth and Tenth Five-Year Plans, the success of the selected programs would be measured in terms of tons of output of petroleum, cubic meters of natural gas, numbers of autos and trucks, kilograms of meat, etc. However, the aggregative importance of performance in these sectors transcends their immediate targets. The sufficiency of the Soviet energy supply from all sources is closely tied to the Soviet planned output of oil and gas.[13] In the Soviet Union, as elsewhere, more energy may be provided by the sources of the technological past, such as low-grade, underground coal, or the sources

10 A. Bergson, "Toward a New Growth Model," *Problems of Communism,* Mar.–Apr. 1973, pp. 1–9.

11 D. B. Diamond, "Principal Targets and Central Thesis of the Ninth Five-Year Plan," in *Analysis of the USSR's 24th Party Congress and Ninth Five-Year Plan,* ed. Norton T. Dodge (Mechanicsville, Md.: Cremona Press, 1971), p. 48; U.S., Central Intelligence Agency, *The Soviet Economy in 1973: Performance, Plans, and Implications,* July 1974.

12 See *Soviet Economic Prospects for the Seventies,* p. 9. The preliminary 1973 figure is 6.8 percent. See also plan-fulfillment figures for 1973 in *Pravda,* Jan. 26, 1974.

13 J. P. Hardt, "West Siberia: The Quest for Energy," *Problems of Communism,* Apr.–May 1973, pp. 25–36.

of the future, such as nuclear energy. However, it cannot be provided as cheaply or as well. Likewise, broader plans to improve technology in machinery output and to raise the level of capital efficiency are tied to the increased availability of high quality energy. In the Soviet Union, as elsewhere, the availability of energy per man-hour or machine-hour worked is considered a useful gauge of industrial productivity, and energy consumption per capita is considered a good measure of overall productivity in the economy.[14] Indeed, in the Soviet Union the ratio of the GNP to the total population, and the level of energy consumption per capita, are both about half of what they are in the United States. It is fair to note that energy consumption does not ensure increased productivity. Appropriate machinery, metal, and skilled labor inputs are required. But Soviet planners may well be correct in considering their oil and gas energy supply as a key bottleneck.

Before assessing the Soviet ability to meet oil and gas requirements in future years, we must say something about the expanding foreign and domestic requirements. The ambitious Ninth Five-Year Plan for petroleum and gas output may prove to be barely adequate for meeting the Soviet domestic, East European, and modest export requirements. The shortfalls in Soviet output in 1972 were kept to a minimum largely by expansion of the West Siberian fields and Middle Eastern oil imports.[15] But requirements are likely to run ahead of expanding supplies after 1975 if the foreign capital and technology are not available to supplement Soviet expansion efforts. By 1975 the Soviet Union may become self-sufficient in natural gas supply and may provide a net export surplus—if exports to Western Europe can continue to be offset by imports from Iran and Afghanistan. This pattern of transit or export balancing between the Middle East and Western Europe may be expanded, especially if Soviet arms sales to the Middle East are increased to provide hard currency exchange for Soviet purchases of oil and gas. The expansion of Soviet pipelines and tanker fleets may provide a Soviet alternative to Western tanker transfer. The transport income may be in kind, i.e., additional oil and gas.

The requirements of five East European countries (East Germany, Poland, Czechoslovakia, Bulgaria, and Hungary) for oil and gas are

14 Baibakov, pp. 82–110.

15 R. W. Campbell, "Some Issues in Soviet Energy Policy for the Seventies," and J. Richard Lee, "The Soviet Petroleum Industry: Promise and Problems," both in *Soviet Economic Prospects for the Seventies*, pp. 50–52, 287 ff.

being met by the Soviet Union through 1975. After that, direct relations with the Middle East may reduce the incremental requirements of Eastern Europe. Completion of a planned pipeline from a port in Yugoslavia would be a significant step toward relieving the Soviet Union of the East European oil drain. However, the East European members of Comecon have invested heavily in Soviet gas and oil transmission facilities and have limited foreign exchange for purchasing Middle Eastern supplies with hard currency. This limits the ability of the East European countries to pay for Middle Eastern oil.

The market for Soviet oil and gas throughout the industrialized world is the nation's most attractive hard currency earner. With a chronic deficiency of hard currency, the Soviet Union would like to continue to have hydrocarbon exports as a major export. However, this prospect is doubtful unless the Soviet Union can restrict its own and East European requirements or step up the expansion of oil and gas output, especially in Siberia. These Siberian developments depend on effective use of Western capital and technology.[16] Expansion of petroleum output is more limited than increases in natural gas output by the availability of proven reserves.

Planning and management efficiency improvements require better statistical information systems, improved mathematically oriented professional economists, and the application of mathematical techniques such as input-output analysis and linear programming. Computer technology and computer systems are central to the effectiveness of these changes. Soviet leaders and planners have apparently decided that Soviet computer technology and skill in computer applications constitute the central consideration or the bottleneck in overcoming Soviet problems in central, regional, and enterprise planning and management efficiency. A national, computer-assisted, statistical information system—the Automated System for Administration of Enterprises and Branches of Industry (ASU)[17]—is being developed as part of the Ninth Five-Year Plan (1971–75). Specific computer applications for air traffic control and terminal operations, industrial processing, etc., have all been given high priority.

[16] Campbell, p. 50; Lee, pp. 287, 288. For an additional view on the link between export ability and outside aid, see Robert W. Campbell, "Siberian Energy Resources and the World Energy Market" (Paper presented at NATO Round Table, Brussels, Jan. 30–Feb. 1, 1974), p. 4.

[17] D. G. Zhimerin, "The Effectiveness of the ASU: Results and Prospects," *Ekonomicheskaya gazeta*, no. 2 (Jan. 1972), pp. 8, 9.

Improved automotive transport is directly and indirectly important to consumer satisfaction. Truck transport is closely correlated to the increasing supply of consumer durables as well as the more complex locational requirements of Soviet producer goods industries. The passenger car offers an attractive form of consumer incentive. Indeed, passenger cars and meat seem to play a special role in current Soviet plans to stimulate increased labor productivity through material incentives. The plans of the 1960s emphasizing substantial increases in money income and a broad expansion of consumer goods output did not appear to be successful. In fact, the rise of personal savings may be interpreted largely as nonspending rather than saving for future purchases.[18] The more critical buyers market that emerged in the 1960s in consumer appliances such as television sets, radio, and kitchen equipment presumably reflected the buyers' resistance to persistently low quality. Sellers markets still persist for passenger cars, meat, and housing space. Although housing may be the number one concern of the Soviet citizen, material improvement in the lot of the average urban dweller appears too expensive for Soviet planners to address at this time.[19] However, cars and meat run close to housing in popularity, and the Soviet leadership has made them primary targets in their plans. There appears to be no problem for either product to clear the market at any price—the current sellers market in passenger cars and meat will continue for some time. Cars are especially attractive, and the Zhiguli, the Soviet version of the Fiat, has become the standard new car. A price many times the average annual wage of an industrial worker and a several years' wait seem to be no barrier to sales.[20] Even the extreme scarcity of adequate repair facilities and limited road networks apparently provide no current sales problem. Likewise, meat quality or assortment at almost any price is clearly no sales problem. Meat from every part of the animal except "the horns and the hoofs" is sold at high prices by American standards in even the best-stocked Moscow stores, demonstrating to

18 David W. Bronson and Barbara S. Severin, "Soviet Consumer Welfare: The Brezhnev Era," in *Soviet Economic Prospects for the Seventies,* p. 381.

19 The official planned increase from 11 cubic meters per urban dweller in 1970 to 11.9 in 1975 seems extremely modest. *Baibakov,* p. 305.

20 The recent lottery listed the Soviet-made Moskvich at 9,200 rubles (*Sotsialisticheskaya industriya,* Jan. 13, 1974). If paid in cash, this represents an outlay of about ten times the per capita real disposable money income in 1972 of 989 rubles per annum (Bronson and Severin, p. 380). Also, the Moskvich is considered inferior to the Zhiguli. Normally, the Soviet-built Moskviches and Volgas are listed at 5,000 and 9,000 rubles, respectively.

even the casual visitor the inelastic nature of the Soviet citizens' demand for meat.[21] To put it more technically, there is little price elasticity and considerable income elasticity for cars and meat in the Soviet Union. If material incentives are able to provide a significant stimulus to labor productivity, meeting the ambitious goals in car and meat output should contribute to this end. Moreover, with the severe constraint on output from the Soviet labor supply shortage, any shortfall in the planned increase in labor productivity will be directly reflected in reduced output.

Commercial Relations and Bottlenecks in the Plan

Accepting, therefore, the importance of energy supply, computer-related systems, automotive production, and animal husbandry systems in Soviet plans, let us examine these economic activities in terms of specifically how Soviet planners are moving to meet their goals, assisted by foreign technology and products, revised domestic priorities, and reform.

Energy Systems

Even with some of the major untapped hydrocarbon resources in the world, the Soviet Union is likely to have shortfalls in energy supplies well before 1980 without substantial foreign capital and technology. J. Richard Lee provides us with more specific details on the Soviet need for foreign oil and gas technology to fill the planned requirements:

It appears that achievement of the original 1975 target for production of 496 million tons of crude oil is doubtful and that attainment of the goal of 320 billion cubic meters of natural gas will be impossible.

The difficulties of exploiting the impressive reserves stem not only from the hostile natural conditions but also from poor planning and organization and a lag in technology. The U.S.S.R. lacks sophisticated geophysical tools, such as modern seismic equipment and computerized field units, used routinely in the West. Without such equipment Soviet capability to locate deep structures is limited. Poor quality drilling equipment also is a bottleneck. Shortages of good quality pipe for drilling and casing, poor quality drill bits, and underpowered mud pumps are among the items that con-

---

[21] U.S., Congress, Senate, Report by H. Humphrey and H. Bellmon to the Agriculture Committee, *Observations on Soviet and Polish Agriculture*, 93d Cong., 1st sess., Jan. 1973 (hereafter *Observations on Soviet and Polish Agriculture*).

tribute to inefficient operations in the field. Heavy reliance on the turbodrill, which is very inefficient below 8,000 feet, has contributed to rising costs and reduced drilling rates as depths of wells increase. Because of the lack of treating facilities in the field, large volumes of associated gas—some 12 billion cubic meters per year—are being flared, a particularly wasteful practice. These and other shortcomings in Soviet technology and equipment have led the U.S.S.R. during the past two or three years to turn to Western suppliers for much needed technical know-how and modern equipment.[22]

In time the rich Soviet oil and gas reserves may be brought into production. But time is of the essence. The full and efficient exploitation of the Vrenyoi natural gas deposits in the West Siberian Arctic is a case in point. Although the Soviets are proceeding on their own, with foreign involvement the time factor would be reduced and the quality of processes significantly improved.[23] Facilities for processing natural gas for export, i.e., for the liquefication process, are also needed. New pipelines for gas transmission to Western Europe and the Scandinavian countries are to provide a major source of hard currency earnings by 1980. But the Soviet Union is still a net importer of gas from Iran and Afghanistan.

In order to make effective use of the foreign capital goods and technology, considerable Soviet infrastructure investment would be required: for example, investment in site development, workers' facilities, rail and water transport facilities, refinery capacity, petrochemical plants. The lack of adequate investment to effectively utilize regional energy development would keep the Soviets from meeting the oil and gas requirements of its domestic economy and those of Eastern Europe, and from being able to export these resources for hard currency. Plans for expanding the gas transmission network to meet the needs of Moscow and Leningrad, the East European countries, members of the Common Market, and the Scandinavian countries could be scaled down or deferred, but not without cost in domestic growth and foreign exchange. Limited investment projects have also led to costly delays in past domestic Soviet development.

A case study of the impact of a limited investment approach to energy development is provided by the East Siberian hydroelectric grid developed in the mid-1960s. At considerable cost, one of the largest hydroelectric projects (Bratsk—with about a 4-million-kilowatt

22 P. 285.
23 See T. Shabad, *Soviet Geography*, Jan. 1975.

capacity) was completed during the Seven-Year Plan (1959–65). Only now, in the Ninth Five-Year Plan, is the industrial load—facilities for nonferrous metal processing, chemical facilities, etc.—being constructed to even supply and demand for power.[24] The cost of limiting investment to a narrow energy production capability without systematic regional development is thus well illustrated. The Soviets have had underutilized hydrocapacity in East Siberia for over a decade. The lesson the Soviet planners may draw is that without regional development of West Siberian industry—including new refineries and a communal and industrial infrastructure—foreign capital and technology will fall short of their potential for solving Soviet energy problems and stimulating econome growth.

Soviet planners may likewise choose to retain their old energy balance method of planning and management in the West Siberian oil and gas development. However, they might be better served to adopt the computer-assisted systems, so well developed and applied by Western petroleum companies, to maximize deliveries and minimize costs.[25] To call such a system market-simulating or an economic reform might be misleading. However, it can be accurately termed a more modern, systematic, and pragmatic approach. Although the regional Party economic sections and the ministries in Moscow might find regional development more difficult to control and understand, the top leadership might appreciate the improved performance.

Computer-related Systems

Computer production and applications are central to Soviet efforts to improve the efficiency of planning and management. Agreements with firms such as Control Data Corporation are designed to bridge the gap between Soviet second- and American fourth-generation computers and to improve the quality of computer applications.[26] Use of computer systems in specific sectors such as air traffic control, bookings of Aeroflot, the petroleum industry, and port operations, is

---

[24] J. P. Hardt, "Industrial Investment in the USSR," in U.S., Congress, Joint Economic Committee, *Comparisons of United States and Soviet Economies*, 86th Cong., 1st sess., Sept. 1959, pp. 132–36; for plan directives, see *Pravda*, Apr. 7, 1971; T. Shabad, *Soviet Geography*, Apr. 1972, p. 261.

[25] Hardt, "West Siberia," pp. 32, 33.

[26] G. Ruders, "Soviet Computers: A Historical Survey," *Soviet Cybernetics Review*, Jan. 1970, pp. 6–44; "Moscow Invites American Companies to Invest in Soviet Industry," *Washington Post*, Aug. 23, 1973; Zhimerin, pp. 8–9.

one type of application.[27] But the major computer application approach is toward the national system of economic reporting.[28]

With a modified American export control policy and an ambitious Soviet production effort, it appears that the Soviet Union may be able to reach the current world level of computer technology. Moreover, available software and peripheral equipment technology may be acquired to apply techniques successfully used in U.S. computer applications. Even if the Soviets catch up in computer technology, this may not lead to keeping up. However, the cost of a modest computer lag may not be serious.

The Soviet investment in computer hardware production related to the national reporting system alone will be substantial, perhaps the equivalent of several billion dollars.[29] Computer applications in industrial and other economic enterprises would likewise absorb large quantities of high quality resources.

A reform in the system of planning and management is probably more important to performance than computer hardware is. Relevant to the effectiveness of the new computer-assisted reporting system is the quality of the data and economic statistics, their use in modern analytic frameworks, and their application by economists and statisticians familiar with modern econometric techniques. Soviet statistical data, even when reported in physical units, are not subject to standard reporting procedures but are subject to bias from the reporters with a built-in inclination to improve the reported statistics

27 V. Glushkov, cited in *Pravda*, Feb. 10, 1973; *Sotsialisticheskaya industriya*, July 8, 1973.

28 E. G. Yakovenko, *Avtomatizirovannye sistemy upravleniya v narodnom khozyaystve SSSR* (Moscow, 1972); V. V. Yakovlev, "Automated Control Systems Effectiveness Is below Expectations," *Ekonomika i organizatsiya promyshlennogo proizvodstva*, no. 4 (1972), pp. 38–50; N. S. Zenchenko, and V. M. Ivanov, "On the Use of Economic-Mathematical Methods and Computers in the National Economy of the RSFSR," *Ekonomika i matematicheskiye metody*, no. 6 (1972), pp. 808–12; Dmitriy Zhimerin, "OGAS—The Electronic Brain," *Pravda*, Aug. 12, 1972; "Problems of Automation and Control of the National Economy," *Ekonomicheskaya gazeta*, no. 50 (1971), pp. 5–6; "Urgent Problems," *Sotsialisticheskaya industriya*, Sept. 23, 1971; Gertrude E. Schroeder, "Recent Developments in Soviet Planning and Incentives," *Soviet Economic Prospects for the Seventies*, pp. 11–38.

29 D. A. Allakhverdyan, "Problems of National Economic Management in the Current Stage," *Finansy SSSR*, no. 11 (1972), pp. 26–36; M. Rakovskiy, "The Potential of Automated Equipment," *Sotsialisticheskaya industriya*, May 21, 1972; and Zhimerin, "Effectiveness of the ASU." Cf. "IBM's $5 Billion Gamble," *Fortune*, Sept. 1966, pp. 118–23.

on which they are judged.[30] The monetary statistics are subject to all the vagaries of the Soviet price system. Conflicts among the various units producing and using statistics such as the Central Statistical Administration, the State Planning Committee, and the various ministries (including those involved in defense production) all tend to perpetuate a system of statistical heterogeneity and uncertainty. Control of statistics—always a source of bureaucratic influence—is still assisted by Soviet criminal law restrictions on release of wide ranges of data usually in the public domain in other countries.

With better data Soviet input-output tables prepared for 1959 and 1966, and scheduled for 1972, might be effectively used in central planning.[31] However, the many professionally trained mathematical economists in institutes such as the Central Economic and Mathematics Institute (TsEMI) in Moscow would probably best be brought into the planning process. A recent call by S. P. Trapeznikov, member of the Party's Central Committee, for academic economists to become more "practical" in their orientation may be a harbinger of some melding of the modernist and traditional planning and economic cadres.[32] Certainly the more than 700 professionals in TsEMI might be more effectively utilized in actual planning at the State Planning Committee. Perhaps the formulation of the forthcoming Fifteen-Year Plan (1975–90) will provide the occasion for integrating input-output and forecasting techniques, improved statistics, professional economists, and computer-assisted systems.[33] The national computer-assisted system in this context might materially improve planning efficiency. Without these critical preconditons of better data, better analytic tools, and professionalism, it might be another expensive example of the classic "garbage-in garbage-out system."

On the enterprise, or sector, level the same preconditions are necessary, but with perhaps more variations in effectiveness. A computer-assisted booking system for Aeroflot would probably be a significant improvement over the present system and would involve little change in information systems, staffing, or analytic approaches. However, managerial systems for handling mill-to-smelter, well-to-refinery,

30 V. G. Treml and J. P. Hardt, eds., *Soviet Economic Statistics* (Durham, N.C.: Duke University Press, 1972), *passim*.

31 V. Vorobyshev, "On the Application of Input-Output Methods in Planning Practice," *Planovoe khoziaistvo*, no. 7 (July 1973), pp. 55–58.

32 "Improving the Role of Economic Science in Communist Constitution," *Ekonomicheskaya gazeta*, no. 1 (Jan. 1974), pp. 3–4.

33 Vorobyshev.

port operation, and other classic operations research problems might require more than standard computer routines to maximize effectiveness. The recent Soviet emphasis on computer time-sharing suggests that problems such as process control and industrial scheduling may be greatly assisted but not necessarily solved by the proper computer hardware and peripheral equipment.[34] A sage Western observer once noted that the best approach to efficient computer usage would be to design the operation as if it were to be converted to computer application and then stop short of conversion. This seems to be the opposite of current Soviet thinking, which is likely to overemphasize the adoption of the latest computer hardware and underemphasize the change in institutions required to make effective use of the computer technology.

Automotive Systems

The Soviet transportation system was designed to handle priority military and heavy industrial products and raw materials. In the past an emphasis on major rail lines, river barges, and selected air transport was to suffice. Now it is recognized that there is a need for a system of transportation—if not interregional, at least intraregional, and especially in the environs of the major cities—to move consumer goods and facilitate personal travel. Soviet planners have acknowledged the need for more trucks and passenger cars. The former are needed to market quality foods, consumer durables, and other products important to a rising real income; the latter, to provide an important part of the incentive increment for more affluent consumers.

Many of the Soviet automotive works still bear signs of their technological origin—the Detroit of the 1930s. Their comparative advantage appeared to be in their capability for conversion to military output. The decision to bring in the Italian Fiat Company in 1966 seems to have been an admission that Soviet-designed cars would not fill the new requirements. Likewise, the major expansion of truck production on the Kama is now being based on American and European technology and equipment. In many cases the most technologically advanced variants were chosen. Technology transfer presumably reflects a gap between Soviet and Western practice and a desire to reduce the time required for indigenous progress.

The importation of production equipment from foreign countries has not been enough. It apparently is also considered necessary not

[34] *New York Times,* Jan. 6, 1974.

only to update Soviet industry by obtaining machinery and process descriptions but to bring in the management of foreign companies to participate in the construction and production of facilities for cars and trucks. Fiat is scheduled to terminate its role in management of the Volga-based auto plant around 1975.[35] American engineers have been working at the construction site of the massive Kama truck plant and will presumably participate in getting the plant into full operation.[36]

The resource priority question does not emerge so clearly in the production of the automotive industry as it does in the broader implications of the automotive age for the Soviet economy. An attempt may be made to use more trucks and autos on the grossly inadequate Soviet road system, with its deficiencies in repair and maintenance facilities; or some effort may be made to provide for these broader needs.[37] A road network and support facilities comparable to those in Western Europe, Japan, and the United States would require a significant infrastructure investment. But will more trucks and cars alone serve the needs of the Soviet economy for long without adequate roads and repair facilities? The answer seems clearly, not for long.

Animal Husbandry Systems

The ambitious meat production goals of the current Five-Year Plan (involving an increase of one-quarter in the per capita meat output) may be met.[38] If they are, commercial relations with the United States will have played a critical role. Certainly a large portion— perhaps as much as half—of the grain purchases made in 1972 was intended to keep Soviet livestock alive.[39] Soviet agricultural managers, having survived the agricultural disaster of 1972, can meet their targets if they can only reach the efficiency levels common in U.S. agribusiness.[40]

35 Imogene U. Edwards, "Automotive Trends in the U.S.S.R.," in *Soviet Economic Prospects for the Seventies*, p. 296.

36 *Washington Post*, May 27, 1973.

37 Edwards, pp. 291–315.

38 Baibakov, p. 300.

39 An estimated half of the Soviet imports, 15–18 million tons, were to fulfill livestock feed grain requirements. *Soviet Economic Outlook*, p. 94.

40 *Observations on Soviet and Polish Agriculture*, pp. 6, 7; U.S., Dept. of Agriculture, *National and State Livestock-Feed Relationships*, by George C. Allen and Margaret Devers, ERS Statistical Bulletin 446, Feb. 1970; N. Burlakov, "Effektivnost proizvodstva produktsii zhivotnovodstva," *Ekonomika selskogo khoziaistva*, no. 5 (1972); U.S., Dept. of Agriculture, *Livestock Feed Balances for the USSR*, by

For this transition, high-protein feed grain and soybeans, breeder stock, and better disease control are all necessary. However, the Soviets appear to be emulating the organization and scale of the massive U.S. feeder lot operations without the complex U.S. supply and distribution systems. Animal husbandry complexes, large poultry farms, and agricultural-industrial associations are being pushed officially to consolidate or replace collective and state farms.[41] Certainly the multimillion-dollar U.S. feeder lots can be very productive and efficient in the American economy. However, even in the United States their efficiency depends on a complex interplay of market supply and distribution systems. The availability of feed, its proper mixing, the removal of manure, and the slaughtering, storage, and distribution systems all must be coordinated. Even in the highly developed U.S. economy, that efficiency assumption does not always prove valid. In Soviet agriculture this kind of foreign agribusiness industrial efficiency would be novel.

The infrastructure for animal husbandry elsewhere has been tied to the improvement of motor transport and of techniques for processing, storing, and handling materials. In Western Europe the rise in motor freight transport in the 1950s paralleled the increase in refrigerated warehouse space and improvements in techniques for handling materials. More recently, refrigerated motor transport has been burgeoning.[42] The infrastructure for meat processing and marketing might seem expensive, but the effectiveness of the Soviet priority of animal husbandry in meat marketing would seem to be at stake.

The Choice: Modernization and Economic Growth, or Traditionalism and Stalinist-type Control

In order to increase the output of energy, computers, trucks, cars, and meat rapidly and more efficiently, greater Soviet reliance on a foreign-technology bridge seems necessary. Conceivably, Soviet strategy on adoption of technology to special needs might run the gamut

Donald Chrisler, ERS Foreign 355; S. Dudin, "Razvivat miasnoe skotovodstvo," *Ekonomika selskogo khoziaistva*, no. 2 (1971).

41 *Pravda*, Dec. 16, 1973, Jan. 26, 1974.

42 Philip M. Raup, "Constraints and Potentials in Agriculture," *The Changing Structure of Europe* (Minneapolis: University of Minnesota Press, 1969), pp. 126–70.

from a full reliance on insulated foreign technology to a full integration of foreign technology with foreign priorities and systems
of economic decision-making. A direct challenge to the traditional,
Stalinist system—the maximum political change variant, or "collapse
theory"—may appear most advantageous economically, but such an
action would call for probably unacceptable changes in the political
and institutional arrangements of the Soviet economy. As suggested
above, combinations of change maximizing economic gain while
minimizing political cost may be increasingly explored by Soviet planners; they may move from the "costless" approach position to a
gradual or measured acceptance of political cost in order to attain
economic benefit. In each of the key economic areas discussed above,
there are variants that seem to combine modernization and improved
economic efficiency within the acceptable precepts of the Soviet
system in a flexible and pragmatic way. Examples of possibly acceptable blends of foreign technology, revised priorities, and reform
are summarized in the following:

1. *For oil and natural gas.* A regional, energy-oriented development
of West Siberia, planned by professional economists (such as Agan-
begian, at the Academy of Sciences in Novosibirsk) and administered
by a regional authority like a modern TVA or a multinational corporation, could be initiated. The systems approach to regional
planning has been advocated by those at the Academy of Sciences in
Novosibirsk and also by S. A. Orudzhev, minister of the Gas Industry.[43] The Novosibirsk staff of mathematically oriented economists
would presumably use techniques commonly employed by Western
multinational companies in foreign operations. Foreign involvement
of Western corporations, such as the consortium presently negotiating
the development of the North Star natural gas project in West
Siberia, would tend to encourage this type of modern, systematic
regional approach. Administratively, the approach might be handled
by a large Soviet production association reporting directly to the
Council of Ministers and the State Planning Committee and/or
through the appropriate ministries and regional Party organs. This
might place the new administrative organization within accepted
political bounds.

Although the large share of resources from planned investment
for the region might require a diversion from the defense sector,

[43] See Hardt, "West Siberia," pp. 32, 33; *Ekonomicheskaya gazeta*, no. 6 (Feb.
1974), p. 7.

another approach to administration would be extension of the Ministry of Defense Industries to special areas such as energy in West Siberia.[44] The efficiency of output, supply, and distribution common to the military sector might be carried over to priority civilian sectors. The military-industrial complex in the Soviet Union would retain its administrative authority even if many of the resources were for nonmilitary purposes.

2. *For computer usage.* A computer-assisted central planning system utilizing input-output methods implemented by high quality data and manipulated by professional economists might be developed —initially for direct use in the long-run planning process, i.e., in the development of the new Fifteen-Year Plan (1976–90). More computer-assisted operations research might be introduced in activities in which foreign technology is dominant. A useful mathematical format for facilitating a transformation from the old planning method to a modernized approach might be the development of the new Fifteen-Year Plan using the input-output table now being prepared for 1972. The data problems delaying the adoption of the previous tables to the annual plan and five-year plans might be resolved in the longer-term program.[45] Some discussion of using projections in the new plan and of limiting planning data to more reliable and homogeneous aggregative data (if they can be developed) also might assist the transitions.[46] As the national information system came into being, it could be helpful in a transition to more modernized, optimal planning for annual and five-year plans. Moreover, this kind of transition might conceivably be accommodated within the current State Planning Committee structure, already very much attuned to computer applications.[47]

A wider application of computer-assisted systems to linear programming of transport, locational, and industrial processing problems

[44] See *Pravda*, Jan. 15, 1970, for decree referring to the role of the Ministry of Defense Industries in the development of energy in West Siberia.

[45] Vorobyshev, p. 56.

[46] Ibid., p. 58.

[47] N. Lebedinskiy, a deputy chairman of Gosplan in charge of computer applications in planning, stated, at a session with the U.S. Congressional Joint Economic Committee in October 1973, that probability would now be incorporated in planning. He referred to variations in foreign trade and weather as factors that could not be controlled in future plans. See also N. Fedorenko and S. Shatalin, "On Problems of Optimal Planning," *Voprosi ekonomiki*, no. 6 (1969); N. Fedorenko, "To Perfect a System of Socialist Planning," *Ekonomika i matematicheskiye metody*, no. 7 (1971).

has long been attractive. An increase in such applications of operations research would seem to be possible within the current institutional framework.[48]

3. *For trucks and passenger cars.* An automotive-transport system designed to accommodate modern motor-freight vehicles as well as passenger cars might be designed and put into the plan. The Soviet transport system, as judged by passenger service and civilian freight deliveries, is, to say the least, not a model of efficiency. However, with higher resource priorities, it seems conceivable that a national highway system, expanded repair and service facilities, and a motor-freight transit authority might operate with reasonable efficiency. The major constraint on entering the automobile age would appear to be the enormous infrastructure resource cost. The cost of the interstate system in the United States, spanning three time-zones, would approximate a minimum cost for a Soviet system that would cover up to eleven time-zones from its western to its eastern extremities and include some very hostile terrain.

4. *For meat.* An animal husbandry system based on a decentralized incentive system of production and a modern centralized system of feed supply, processing, and distribution of meat products might be more productive economically than the current animal husbandry complexes, without being politically unacceptable. Two adjustments may be necessary in the current Soviet institutional approach: (1) a shift to a small-scale approach to the agricultural-industrial associations or animal husbandry complexes *within* the Soviet collective farm system; (2) an even greater allocation of investment resources to the development of a rural infrastructure to improve the supply, storage, and distribution systems of the animal husbandry complexes.

The criticisms of this small-scale operation have been largely political. Genady Voronov, who was dropped from the Politburo after the Party Congress in 1971, favored agricultural dependence on incentives through the "link system" of organization in collective agriculture. The application of the *beznariadnoe zveno* (unstructured link) system to animal husbandry would involve continuous involvement of a selected group of peasants, for example, an extended family, to the care of livestock. This might be combined with central supply, processing, and distribution facilities. Alec Nove's comments in 1970 seem to make even more sense today:

48 B. Ward, "Linear Programming and Soviet Planning," in *Mathematics and Computers in Soviet Economic Planning,* ed. J. P. Hardt et al. (New Haven: Yale University Press, 1967), pp. 147–200.

The future? The leadership well knows that massive investments will be necessary in farm equipment, roads, trucks, electric power, amenities, irrigation, drainage, and the distribution trades. Plans do provide for this, but progress will be necessarily slow and expensive. One wonders what could be achieved by harnessing peasant initiative, through the *zveno* and similar small joint enterprises (one critic has proposed giving the autonomous *zveno* the time-honored designation of artel). More autonomy in farm management, and a less irrational price system, would also cost little. However, in its present mood the leadership seems unwilling to launch major experiments.[49]

The system of small-scale incentives within the current institutional structure has done well in Estonia. Moreover, this approach seems to be similar to an effective animal husbandry program now in vogue in Poland, even though Polish agriculture is no longer collectivized.[50] The current model is the highly centralized Moldavian agriculture, which has in the past come under considerable criticism.

Economic necessity may pressure the leadership for change, but established institutional pressures will resist any aggregative improvement that may adversely influence either Party power or political performance.[51] The direct involvement of the Party in economic decision-making and staffing is critical. If the Politburo feels that economic modernization leaves it in charge of the economic "commanding heights," it may be willing to withdraw the local Party from the detailed decision-making powers it has insisted the local Party have in the past. If economic performance did not deteriorate while changes were occurring, this Party withdrawal might continue. At the same time withdrawal of the Party would be limited. The Party *apparatchiki* at all levels have exercised control over appointments to key economic positions, rewards, punishments, etc., through the *nomenklatura* system.[52] Modification of this power to that of a veto

---

49 A. Nove, "Soviet Agriculture under Brezhnev," *Slavic Review*, Sept. 1970, p. 410.

50 *Observations on Soviet and Polish Agriculture*, pp. 17, 18; W. Lipski, "Changes in Agriculture," in *Gierek's Poland*, ed. A. A. Bromke and J. W. Strong (New York: Praeger, 1973), pp. 101–7.

51 J. Hardt, D. Gallik, and V. Treml, "Institutional Stagnation and Changing Economic Strategy in the Soviet Union," in U.S., Congress, Joint Economic Committee, *New Directions in the Soviet Economy*, 89th Cong., 2d sess., 1966, pp. 19–62.

52 J. Hough, "The Party *Apparatchiki*," and J. P. Hardt and T. Frankel, "The Industrial Managers," both in *Interest Groups in Soviet Politics*, ed. H. G. Skilling and F. Griffiths (Princeton: Princeton University Press, 1971), pp. 47–92, 171–208.

might be acceptable, whereas elimination of past prerogatives might be unacceptable.

The military has always occupied the preferred position in terms of resource allocation. Ministries of the defense industries have been the most favored and, not surprisingly, the most efficient. Modernization and professionalism nonetheless receive support in the military from those who may favor their own control of their support industries over the Party control. Still, acceptance of professionalism does not imply that a diminution of both military resource claims and control would be welcome. Moreover, continued military control might be in the interest of efficiency. The shift in priority to civilian investment and consumer goods output may benefit by the superior efficiency of the military operation rather than by the traditional management in civilian sectors. One method for shifting priorites but retaining the efficiency of the defense industry enterprises would be to have the military managerial sector of the economy take over more of the civilian tasks. The statement of Aleksei Kosygin that an increasing share of the consumer goods was being produced in defense plants may be indicative of this kind of approach.[53] The role of the military builders in civilian construction has long been established. In Moscow alone many museums, university buildings, airport facilities, and industrial workers' apartments are accomplishments of the military builders.[54] An extension of the production and construction under military aegis to the regional energy projects might be appealing from the standpoint of short-term efficiency and minimum institutional change. It is less likely that military administration would be as effective in the consumer goods area. A danger that Party Secretary Brezhnev would have to evaluate in increasing the military span of control within the civilian economy would be the possibility of independence from Party control. Moreover, the military "vote" in Party councils would be increased, perhaps at the expense of civilian Party *apparatchiki*.

Historical evidence suggests that important changes in policy occur in the Soviet body politic only under the pressure of crises. The institutional resistance to change in resource allocation policy and reform is very strong. For purposes of illustrating the type of crises that might lead to change, let us assume the following: that the completion of the Ninth Five-Year Plan has been heralded by opera-

[53] *Pravda*, Apr. 7, 1971.
[54] A. I. Romashko, *Military Builders in the Construction Projects of Moscow* (Moscow: Voennoe izdatel'stvo, Ministry of Defense Press, 1972).

tion of a new computer-assisted planning system (ASU) and a significant increase in meat availability; that financing foreign trade has become closely tied to petroleum and natural gas exports to hard currency countries; and that auto and truck output has filled the Soviet roads with motor transport. Then the economic problems begin to get serious: not only does the new, expensive computer-assisted system have problems in coming to full operation, but it becomes increasingly clear that the data and analysis problems must be solved before the ASU can be effective; weather—the chronic crisis generator for all Russian leaders—turns bad, causing the maintenance of livestock herds to become a problem, and the long-run program for increasing meat supply is thereby jeopardized; weather and technological problems delay the tapping of new sources of oil and gas, and domestic energy shortages develop; finally, the inadequate Soviet road network is strained to the breaking point—traffic jams and supply problems become chronic. Of course, this is all exaggerated to illustrate the worst case. But a combination of the above-noted problems in various degrees is possible, if not likely. Who would be held responsible is very uncertain. But in my view the possibility for change would be enhanced by such crises.

Change Involving Less Threat and More "Peaceful Coexistence"

Were the Soviet leaders to opt for flexible, pragmatic means of improving economic performance, there might be a shift in the international competition between the superpowers, from military to economic confrontation, and the likelihood of a more stable, peaceful world community might be enhanced. Were the competition on peaceful grounds more open, exchanges might be possible with less of a requirement for an iron curtain or armed camp approach. In the cold war security context, economic information was viewed primarily as intelligence; personal and professional exchanges, as potential sources of subversion or espionage. The past psychology has been that each side's gain should be the other's loss, that is, zero sum. Increasing commercial relations, emphasizing technological exchange, might provide a vehicle for change in the international environment and might lead to increased communications between the Communist and non-Communist systems.[55] Both economic systems might well change, but not necessarily toward convergence. Economic informa-

55 *U.S.-Soviet Commercial Relations,* pp. 1–14.

tion might come to be viewed as requiring more mutual marketing needs. Professional and personal exchanges might be viewed as mutually advantageous. Expanding commercial relations have been associated with accommodation and change in the institutional framework of both the Soviet and the American body politic. This is probably unlikely. Even though economic priority and institutional changes may result to maximize the advantages of technology transfer, a revolution in the system as a whole does not seem necessary or likely. If, by pragmatic, ad hoc measures, flexible accommodations cannot be made to improve efficiency without endangering the central features of the Party control system, the leaders will probably stop short.

Pressures for Change in the Soviet Institutions

In 1945 Stalin permitted the Soviet Union to join the United Nations, but not the economic organizations connected with it—the International Monetary Fund, the International Bank for Reconstruction and Development (the World Bank), etc. The reason, presumably, was that these international economic associations would lead to economic dependence on the West, as well as to unwelcome outside leverage on Soviet policy and institutions. Bilateral aid through the Marshall Plan was also declined, presumably for similar reasons. Other international conventions, treaties, and organizations were likewise avoided, in line with the Stalinist policy of bifurcation of the world economy and self-reliance of the socialist bloc of nations. Copyright and shipping conventions and the General Agreement on Tariffs and Trade (GATT) were not joined or conformed to.

Now Soviet policy has changed, and the U.S.S.R. has begun to accept some of these international relationships—to share in their benefits and accept their constraints. This is part of the official U.S. view of normalization as noted by Under Secretary of State for Economic Affairs William J. Casey:

An increasingly important objective of U.S. policy, as our economic relations with Communist states are normalized, is the encouragement of stable consumer-oriented societies more fully integrated into the international trade and payments system. Only certain Communist countries have sought active participation in this process through membership in the foundation institutions of the international system, the GATT and the IMF-IBRD. There is no reason to expect this situation will alter in the near future.[56]

56 Cited in U.S., Dept. of State, *Bulletin* 68 (May 21, 1973):640.

The changes in the traditional Soviet state trading monopoly, revised economic disclosure systems, and steps to join the institutions of the international financial and commercial communty may have other effects:

1. *Relaxation in the insulation of the Soviet foreign trade sector from the domestic economy.* The foreign economy may not continue to be fully insulated from the domestic Soviet economy. Technology transfer, managerial techniques, concepts of comparative advantages—Western pricing and marketing techniques—may have spillover effects. A special foreign enclave in meat production employing U.S. agribusiness methods, natural gas and oil output consortia using American methods and techniques, and Western-oriented auto and truck facilities—all may have direct and indirect effects. Operating in critical Soviet bottleneck areas, those foreign enclaves may relieve the pressure for economic reform by meeting priority needs. At the same time, pressure may build up among Soviet professionals and interested Party members for wider utilization of Western practices and decentralized contact within the domestic Soviet economy.

2. *Emergence of a Soviet interest group for making export industries a preferred sector.* Pressure may rise for an export industry enclave to meet Western market demands. An export priority in supply and quality control, similar to the traditional military priority, would go far toward meeting the Soviet balance-of-payments problems. It has been suggested that the Soviet economy has a three-tiered priority system, with military industries at the top, the conventional civilian industry in the center, and agricultural and service industries at the bottom. Under balance-of-payments pressure, Soviet export industries might be added just below the defense sector in the priority pyramid. Whether or not export industries could be kept as an insulated priority sector, as the military support facilities have been, is an open question. And it remains to be determined where the skilled management and production manpower would come from and how the priorities would be adjudicated.

3. *Institutional effects of foreign credits and concessionary economics.* The large joint ventures in energy and other raw materials to be financed by Western capital would place the Soviet Union in a debtor's position. The degree of direct involvement in construction and operation of the projects might approach the traditional foreign concessionary status approved by Lenin in the early 1920s. The debtor-creditor relationship and the foreign concessionary status put pressure on each side. Each has leverage over the other: to expand

or modernize on the one hand, or to control and expropriate on the other; to meet commitments and payments, or to protect investments. A regional economic unit in Siberia and the regional Party leaders might develop an export orientation with an affinity toward commercial relations with the United States and Japan, for example.[57]

At the same time, large-scale foreign concerns, especially American, may provide integrated production facilities directly to the Soviet enterprises. One example of this kind of arrangement is the delivery by Phillips International to the R.S.F.S.R. Ministry of State Farms of a wide range of machinery covering all aspects of fodder preparation and distribution and manure removal. American equipment for cattle fattening at Armavir in Krasnodar Krai can accommodate 30,000 head of cattle.[58] Another example is the construction of a new bottling plant for Pepsi-Cola, which began in 1973 after the agreement on the exchange of Pepsi-Cola for vodka. The new plant was to be operating, within the appropriate Soviet ministry, by the end of 1974.[59] These arrangements not only dilute the former monopoly of the Ministry of Foreign Trade but have the potential for setting up interest-group-like pressures in foreign concessionary enclaves.

Pressures for Change in the U.S. Trading System

The prospects of an expanding new American market in the Soviet Union and Eastern Europe tend to promote accommodation with the monopolistic Soviet foreign trading system. Best suited for institutionally dealing with the Soviet state trading monopoly are the large multinational conglomerates with good U.S. government connections. A cooperative Soviet government, by following a policy of limited accreditation, selective contracting, and limited sharing of information, may encourage a privileged and limited relationship with corporations in the United States. Indeed, a barter arrangement, such as Pepsi-Cola for vodka, may provide exclusive access to the Soviet market. The dangers of Western accommodation to the Soviet foreign trade monopoly lie partly in problems arising from constraint of trade. Moreover, as executive government support is involved, as well as congressional review of trade legislation, the attendant secrecy in private company–Soviet government relations may limit appro-

[57] An idea first suggested during discussion with Prof. Gregory Grossman.

[58] *Moscow Domestic Service* (in Russian), July 3, 1973; *FBIS* (Soviet Union), July 5, 1973.

[59] *Sotsialisticheskaya industriya*, May 30, 1973.

priate public review of commercial relations. Secrecy in the grain sales in 1972 and subsequent congressional difficulties in piecing together the relevant facts are illustrative of this problem. The monopoly tendency in commercial relations, the restrictive handling of normally public data, and the general modification or dilution of normal international commercial standards in order to accommodate Soviet desires to minimize changes in the Soviet system are among the possible costs or dangers of the newly emerging commercial relationship.

The accommodation to the Soviet state trading system—even though representing important changes and concessions on the part of the Soviet Union—may thus create specific problems for U.S. policymakers.

1. *A Soviet trade lobby in the United States.* The monopolistic joint American-Soviet production and marketing ventures may become a very effective political and economic force in the United States.[60] Pricing and allocation policy to meet the needs of the Soviet economy may effectively compete with the less organized domestic market in the United States. Discrimination *for* the Soviet market, it could be argued, might be an appropriate determination of public policy in some cases. It would be a questionable policy, however, if it were based on the degree of constraint of trade and effective lobbying. It is conceivable, but not likely, that production for the export market, namely, the Soviet Union, might take precedence over production for the domestic market. This criticism, apparently often heard in Japan in terms of its foreign/domestic market priorities, may become relevant to policy considerations in the United States.

2. *The credit and concessionary pressures.* Just as the United States is said to be under pressure from Middle Eastern oil-exporting nations to moderate its foreign policy vis-à-vis Israel, so a credit line to the Soviet Union—i.e., committed investments in Soviet-American joint ventures and some dependence of the U.S. economy on Soviet energy supply—might be a constraining factor on other policies.

The administration's view of mutual vested interests of the United States and the Soviet Union may indeed be accurate. The leverage that each side derives from the new relationship may be offsetting. Moreover, the sum of these counteracting forces may result in a mutual interest in stability and a closer adherence to recognized

[60] Prof. Gregory Grossman first voiced this sentiment at an informal seminar in Washington in April 1973, and later in *Soviet Economic Outlook.*

international economic rules of the game, and thus be mutually beneficial.

However, applying Dupreel's theorem to conflict relations—"The opposing forces tend to balance each other. They take the same forms to meet and neutralize each other more completely"[61]—we may be concerned that in its accommodation to or competition with the Soviet system, the United States may have adversely changed its system of relations with its major trading partners in Europe and Asia. Indeed, some recent U.S. negotiations and policies with Japan and Western Europe have more the hallmarks of the Soviet pattern than of traditional U.S. dealings—for example, secrecy; tough bargaining, interrelating security, political, and economic matters; bilateral state-to-state relations; punitive use of controls and quotas; etc. Thus, the indirect effects of U.S. success in accommodating East-West, Soviet-American views and systems may be a change in U.S. relations with Western nations and a weakening of the beneficial, market orientation of the international economic system.

Even if the détente is viewed as marginal to expanding Soviet-American commercial relations, there are some critical questions to be asked in formulating Western policy. Should the Soviet market receive preferential or "equal and nondiscriminatory" treatment? If the latter, what does it mean? If the same question is asked about credits, what should be the answer? The risks of credit arrangements rise with the length of time of repayment and the degree of involvement in joint ventures with the Soviet Union. Indeed, the leverage of the creditor may be greater than the leverage of the debtor nation, especially after the investment has been made.[62] These terms of commercial relations are negotiable and presumably will be subject to hard bargaining. But whatever bargains are struck, they may be marginal to the overall process of change in the Soviet Union. However, the change in the Soviet Union might have a significant impact on Western foreign policy. Greater concern with domestic economic performance dependent on a continuous supply of Western technology might lead the Soviet Union to become a more responsible member of the international community of nations.

---

[61] Eugene Dupreel, *Sociologie General* (Paris: Presses Universitaires de France, 1948), as cited in Jan F. Triska and David D. Finley, *Soviet Foreign Policy*, (New York: Macmillan, 1968), pp. 284 ff. Cf. J. Wilczynski, "East-West Trade—A Gateway to Convergence," *Economics of Planning* 8, no. 3 (1968):232–51.

[62] Cf. views of various witnesses at Joint Economic Committee hearings, in *Soviet Economy Outlook, passim.*

This possibility of Soviet political change at home carries with it the major expectation of politcal benefit to the United States from expanding its commercial relations with the Soviet Union. Economic gains to the United States in jobs, balance-of-payments benefits, sales, etc., are all likely to be comparatively modest. Selected increased availability of raw materials and the increased sales of a small number of American companies may account for the economic gains. The Soviet Union is not likely to become one of the United States' major or critical trading partners. Probable political gains that might merit paying economic costs or incurring risks on the part of the Western nations, especially the United States, include the following: (1) a reduction of the priority of resource allocation to Soviet military programs, and (2) a degree of economic professionalism in Soviet planning, and of market simulation in management, closer to what is found in Western countries.

This professional opening of the Soviet economy to external influences might fortify the pressures toward reordering priorities and reforming the Soviet system of planning and management.

Some in the West view the linkage among commercial relations, priorities, and reform as "sheer fantasy."[63] Others argue that liberalization abroad and repression at home are the conscious, even inevitable, companion policies of Soviet leaders in détente.[64] Some authoritative Soviet writers appear to view this type of linkage as a form of subversion or perpetration of "cold war views."[65] Viewed as part of a process of superpower negotiation—the détente the liberalizers would argue—perhaps the subversive linkage would be "sheer fantasy." However, if we consider change more narrowly, within the parameters of reviving economic performance as a primary goal of Soviet leadership, the steps necessary to attain the desired results through flexible and pragmatic change become increasingly likely over time. This is not to suggest that the Soviet leadership *must* change the Soviet economic system and revise resource allocation priorities, but rather that the logic may have increasing force and that the leaders' own self-interest dictates this sort of institutional and political change. In this view foreign policy changes such as the détente are more a derivative of domestic change than a primary

63 See, for example, Walter Lacqueur, *New York Times Magazine*, Dec. 16, 1973, p. 100.

64 W. Leonhardt, "The Domestic Politics of the New Soviet Foreign Policy," *Foreign Affairs*, Oct. 1973, p. 70.

65 G. Arbatov, *Pravda*, July 1973.

moving force. Soviet relations with the United States would thus have a marginal effect on discouraging or encouraging domestic Soviet economic change. Moreover, the apparent persistence of Soviet policy toward expanding East-West trade—in spite of bombings of North Vietnam, the Mideast War, possible denial of most-favored-nation tariff treatment and Export-Import Bank credits—is easier to understand if the course of Soviet-American relations is interpreted as a result of Soviet self-interest in economic improvement more than a result of détente politics, summitry, or the personal diplomacy of General Secretary Leonid Brezhnev and Presidents Richard Nixon and Gerald Ford.

Coincident with improved Soviet-American relations is the increasing Soviet concern with the People's Republic of China. China played its United States card with the Soviet Union when it announced U.S.-Chinese rapprochement following the Peking summit. Commercial relations between the United States and the People's Republic of China are growing even more rapidly than U.S.-U.S.S.R. trade. The new course of U.S.-Chinese relations, in turn, influences the emerging pattern of U.S.-Soviet relations and will continue to be a basis for Soviet judgments in conflicts among their domestic resource priorities: defense, civilian investment, and consumption. How important the improvement in international climate resulting from summitry (the détente), the Soviet concern with China, and the Soviet need for Western technology and trade are, as compared with improving economic performance, in the minds of Soviet leaders, is not easy to measure. But Brezhnev's problems and opportunities seem to strengthen the view that economic improvement and trade are his central considerations.

By political and ideological calculus, the revised priorities and reform of the Soviet economy may be viewed as too costly. The resource claims of entrenched bureaucracies and the Party control of economic institutions have been traditional since the first Stalinist Five-Year Plan. The prospect of significant economic gain is a putative basis for Soviet leaders to accept the political costs of change in a system responsible for the past power and success of the Communist Party of the Soviet Union and in entrenched bureaucracies, such as the military, because the future of the current Soviet leadership may depend on its ability to deliver from improved economic performance. The personal gain or loss to General Secretary Brezhnev from changes in economic performance may be more important to the top Soviet leadership than the loss of power and prerogatives of the institutions he controls. This logic would hold if the gains from institutional flexibility in economic policy did not place Brezhnev in personal political jeopardy, but strengthened through a record of improved economic performance his hold on the Party leadership.

The Interaction of Economics
and Japanese Foreign Policy

Young C. Kim

THIS paper is an attempt to delineate the nature of the interaction of economics and foreign policy by examining two cases in Japanese foreign policy. The first case, one of Japanese-Soviet relations, considers the issue of the Northern Territories and Japanese participation in the development of Siberia. The second case concerns the impact of the recent oil crisis on Japan's foreign and security policy.

Case 1

Japanese-Soviet relations in recent years vividly illustrate the interaction of economics and foreign policy. Two of the outstanding issues between these countries have concerned the Northern Territories and Japan's economic cooperation in the development of Siberia. The former is essentially a political question, while the latter is an economic one. The history of Japanese relations with the Soviet Union since the mid-1960s has demonstrated that the two issues are inseparable and exert mutually constraining influences.

The Northern Territories Issue

The termination of a state of war and the resumption of diplomatic relations between Japan and the Soviet Union occurred in the form of the Joint Declaration of 1956. The single obstacle to the conclusion of a peace treaty at that time, and since, has been Japan's claim to the Northern Territories, consisting of Etorofu, Kunashiri, Habomai, and Shikotan. Japan has insisted that the four islands, which came under Soviet occupation in 1945, be returned as a precondition for the signing of a peace treaty.[1]

---

[1] In the Joint Declaration of 1956, the Soviet Union expressed its intention to return two of the islands, Habomai and Shikotan, after the peace treaty was

According to the Soviet view, the territorial issue has long been settled by such international agreements as those concluded in the Crimea and at Potsdam, and by the instruments of Japan's surrender. The Soviet Union further holds that in the San Francisco peace treaty of 1951, Japan renounced its claim to Sakhalin and the Kuriles, including the disputed islands of Etorofu and Kunashiri.[2]

Japan's position is that Etorofu and Kunashiri, together with Habomai and Shikotan, have always been the "inherent territory" of Japan, and that they do not form part of the renounced Kuriles because they had not been acquired by conquest. The Japanese argue that all claims to the Kuriles were renounced by Japan in the peace treaty, but that the Kuriles were not ceded to the Soviet Union. Moreover, they hold that the Soviet Union is not entitled to benefits resulting from the San Francisco treaty because it was not a signatory.[3]

The U.S. government has generally supported the Japanese position. In a September 1956 statement, the State Department expressed the opinion that these four islands have always been part of Japan proper and should in justice be considered as under Japanese sovereignty. It further stated that, despite the Yalta agreement and the San Francisco peace treaty, the legal determination of the status of the territories in question has yet to be made.[4]

In the months following the announcement that Nixon would visit China, the Japanese detected signs of Soviet flexibility on the issue. The Japanese thought it significant that Gromyko, during his visit to Japan in January 1972, refrained from using the familiar expression, "The matter has been settled." The Japanese ascribed this to a desire to woo Japan away from the United States and prevent a Japanese-Chinese rapprochement. An agreement was made at that time for the two nations to begin negotiations on a peace treaty

---

signed. Later, the Soviets added a stipulation that these two islands would not be relinquished unless all foreign troops were withdrawn. At another time, the Soviets hinted that the reversion of Okinawa to Japan might hasten the return of Habomai and Shikotan.

[2] *Pravda*, Sept. 20, 1964, July 26, 1967, July 30, 1970, Nov. 26, 1970; *Izvestia*, Oct. 29, Nov. 13, 1970; Rosemary Hayes, *The Northern Territorial Issue* (Washington, D.C.: Institute for Defense Analysis, 1972), pp. 23–26.

[3] Nampo Doho Engo Kai, *Hoppo Ryodo no Chii*, 1962; Nampo Doho Engo Kai, *Hoppo Ryodo Mondai Shiryoshu*, 1966; Hoppo Ryodo Fukki Kisei Domei, *Hoppo Ryodo no Sho Mondai*, 1967; "Kunashiri, Etorofu Ryoto no Ryoyuken Mondai," *Chosa Geppo*, May 1969, pp. 60–75.

[4] U.S., Dept. of State, *Bulletin* 24, no. 614 (Apr. 9, 1951): 577; 35, no. 900 (Sept. 24, 1956): 484.

before the end of 1972. Japan interpreted this to mean negotiations regarding the territorial question.

Prime Minister Tanaka paid an official visit to the Soviet Union October 7–10, 1973, and discussed, among other items, the Northern Territories issue with Soviet leaders. The joint Japanese-Soviet statement issued on October 10 at the conclusion of the talks deserves close attention for what it contains as well as for what it omits. There is *no* direct reference to the territorial problem in the communiqué. However, the Japanese are firm in their understanding that the territorial problem will be included in future negotiations on a peace treaty.[5]

The key sentences of the communiqué are: "Settlement of outstanding questions, leftover since the time of the Second World War and the signing of a peace treaty, will make a contribution. . . . The two sides agreed to continue the talks on signing a peace treaty between both countries at an appropriate period in 1974."

These sentences clearly indicate to the Japanese a Soviet agreement to hold talks on the territorial issue. In their opinion the phrase "the outstanding questions" refers specifically to the territorial issue. It should be noted that the joint statement mentions outstanding questions. I have been told privately that in the Japanese original draft *question* was in fact in the singular, but was changed at Soviet request, and that Japan has received explicit Soviet assurance that the unsettled questions include the territorial issue. Moreover, as the Japanese argument goes, the single impediment to the peace treaty between the two countries has been precisely this territorial issue. The most conservative and skeptical interpretation would probably indicate that the territorial issue is at least included among the unsettled questions. The Japanese claim that for the first time the top Soviet leaders conceded that the territorial issue exists, and that Japan successfully placed the matter on the agenda for future negotiation. The Japanese see the summit diplomacy of October 1973 as a step forward in the resolution of the territorial problem.[6]

Soviet officials on the other hand insist that there has been no change in their position on the territorial issue. The Soviets believe the Japanese interpretation was advanced for domestic political propaganda and is not warranted. As far as the Soviets are concerned,

[5] *Asahi Shimbun*, Oct. 11, 1973; *Mainichi Shimbun*, Oct. 11, 1973.
[6] *Asahi Shimbun*, Oct. 11, 1973; *Mainichi Shimbun*, Oct. 11, 1973.

unsettled questions do *not* include the territorial question, but refer rather to such questions as "safe fishing." Thus the Soviets dismiss the Japanese interpretation as unfounded and self-serving.

Several major considerations appear to underlie Soviet refusal to relinquish these islands: (1) The Soviets fear that the return of these islands would not wholly satisfy the Japanese—that the Japanese would then demand the northern part of the Kuriles and, eventually, southern Sakhalin as well. (2) The Soviets believe that concession on this matter would open up a Pandora's box—other countries with territorial grievances against the Soviet Union would be encouraged to pursue them. It should be remembered that the People's Republic of China supports Japan's claim to the Northern Territories. This surely enhances Soviet sensitivity to the territorial issue[7]—hence, the Soviet insistence that the post–World War II boundaries remain final. (3) The Soviets feel that time is on their side. The longer the status quo continues (the fact of Soviet control), the greater the validity of the Soviet claim to the islands. Remembering what occurred with the two Germanys, and Soviet relations with them, they believe a day will come when Japan will be resigned to the present boundaries. (4) The Soviet military is reportedly opposed to the return of the disputed territory because of the strategic value of the Kuriles.[8] According to the Soviet navy, the Kuriles (including Etorofu and Kunashiri) constitute a protective shield for the Soviet Far East and provide them with relative security and a convenient access for their operations in the Pacific.

It should be pointed out that the Japanese have no illusions that the Soviets will return the islands. They concede that Soviet fear of adverse repercussions on other territorial claims necessarily figures in Soviet thinking. However, more fundamentally, the Japanese are convinced that the Soviets simply cannot be expected to relinquish any territory already acquired. The question is, then, why do the Japanese continue to raise the issue when they entertain no realistic expectation of return. Several considerations are operating here: (1) The question of territory evokes sensitive nationalistic sentiments, and no politician, including those on the Left, can afford to run counter to this sensitivity. In fact, some opposition parties have made claim to a greater area of the Kuriles than has the ruling Liberal

[7] *Pravda*, Sept. 2, 1964; *Izvestia*, Feb. 4, 1972; *International Affairs* (Moscow), Oct. 1964, p. 80.

[8] Hoppo Ryodo Fukki Kisei Domei, pp. 13–14; *Mainichi Shimbun*, Oct. 12, 1973.

Democratic party.[9] (2) The issue is compounded by Japanese distrust[10] and resentment of the Russians, especially for their unilateral violation of the neutrality pact near the end of World War II.[11] (3) Former residents of the Northern Territories and other groups are agitating for the return of the islands. They do not, however, constitute an important political force, particularly in comparison with the groups that pressured for the return of Okinawa to Japan. But they are nonetheless a force to be reckoned with, potentially powerful to the extent to which they are supported by the political parties and elite opinion. (4) The Japanese government feels that it must keep the issue alive if only to prevent the Soviet government from justifying its control on the basis of uncontested rule.[12] (5) Some Japanese perceive the issue as leverage against the Soviet Union to obtain concessions in other sectors. (6) Some Japanese entertain the hope that the Soviets will be compelled, under a major crisis such as a Sino-Soviet war, to return the islands in exchange for Japanese neutrality.

Japan's Role in the Development of Siberia

Since the mid-1960s, negotiations relating to Japan's involvement in the development of Siberia have yielded some results.[13] Agreements on three projects were concluded during 1968–71: the timber agreement (July 1968), the agreement on the development of Wrangel port (December 1970); and the development of wood chip and pulp production (December 1971).

9 Shigeo Sugiyama, "Diplomatic Relations between Japan and the Soviet Union with Particular Emphasis on Territorial Questions," in *Japan in World Politics*, ed. Young C. Kim (Washington, D.C.: Institute for Asian Studies, 1972), pp. 34–36; *Akahata*, May 20, 1971; *Komei Shimbun*, July 29, 1973; Nihon Shakai to Senkyo Taisaku Iinkai, *So Senkyo Seisakushu*, 1972, p. 32.

10 *Sankei* newspaper poll of Oct. 1972; *Yomiuri* newspaper poll of June 1969; a monthly poll of Jiji press, 1969–72.

11 Oba Shunsuke, "Fuho Senyu sareta Hoppo Ryodo," *Seikai Crai*, June 1972, pp. 62–63; Hanami Tatsumi, "Hoppo Zen Ryodo ga Nihon Reyo da," *Seikai Crai*, Jan. 1970, pp. 40–41; *Hoppo Ryodo no Sho Mondai* (Getsuyo Kai Repoto), Dec. 22, 1969, pp. 18–20.

12 Shigeo Sugiyama, "Ryodo Mondai wa donattaka," *Sekai to Nippon*, Nov. 26, 1973, p. 1.

13 Kiichi Saeki, "Toward Japanese Cooperation in Siberian Development," *Problems of Communism*, May–June 1972, pp. 5–7; D. Petrov and Syrokomskiy, "Fresh Winds over Japan," *Literaturnaya gazeta*, June 6, 1973; N. Nikolayev, "Expansion of Soviet-Japanese Relations," *International Affairs*, Aug., 1973, pp. 42–52.

Under the first agreement Japan was to supply $133 million in equipment and $30 million in consumer goods over a three-year period for development of the timber and wood-working industry on the Amur River. Repayments were to be made in the form of Soviet exports of timber during 1969–73. The terms of Japanese credit for the equipment were a 20-percent deposit with repayment of the balance over a five-year period at 5.8 percent interest. Deferred payments were arranged on Japanese exports of $40 million in consumer goods.

The second project provided for Japanese delivery of equipment, machinery, and materials for the development of Wrangel port in eastern Siberia. Japanese credit of $80 million specified terms of 12 percent down and cash repayment in seven years at 6 percent.

The third agreement stipulated Japan's delivery of modern machinery and equipment for development of wood chip and pulp production with deliveries to Japan for the period 1972–81. Japanese credit of about $45 million was to be repaid over six years at 6 percent interest.

Several projects have been under discussion between Japan and the Soviet Union.[14] One is the development of heavy coking coal in southern Yakutia for the 1974–79 period. Preliminary information indicates that Japanese credit would be around $350 million, with the Soviets supplying Japan about 5 million tons of coal annually beginning in 1980. The initial agreement was reached in Moscow on March 9, 1974. Another project would involve exploiting natural gas in Yakutia and transporting it through pipeline to the Soviet Far East. From there, liquefied natural gas would be carried by tankers to Japan and the United States.

A two-year survey will be financed by credits of $120 to $150 million by Japan and the United States, with the terms of credit to be negotiated later. Japan would supply a bank loan of $1.7 billion concurrent with the same amount of input from U.S. firms for the project.

Other projects include extending the Tyumen oil pipeline, prospecting for oil and gas on the shelf of Sakhalin, developing Udokan copper ore and Buruktal nickel, as well as a second general agreement on the development of timber resources. The Tyumen project is considered by both sides as the most important. For this project Japan would provide over a billion dollars in credit for pipe and

[14] *Nihon Keizai Shimbun*, Mar. 9, 1973; *Asahi Shimbun*, June 23, 1973; Saeki, pp. 7–11.

other equipment to extend the existing pipeline from Tyumen to Irkutsk (4,100 miles) and on to Nakhohodka (2,600 miles). Japan would be supplied with about 25 million tons a year of crude oil for twenty years.

Major objectives are discernible in Soviet developmental plans. The Soviet Union is determined to establish major economic complexes extending from European Russia to Siberia to provide Soviet industry with the necessary fuel and raw materials by utilizing the resources there. The Soviets anticipate earning foreign currency and importing advanced machinery and consumer goods by exporting these Siberian resources. European Russia may be partially relied upon to assist in the development of western Siberia, but eastern Siberia and the Far East pose major problems in terms of transporting the necessary machinery, construction material, and consumer goods—hence the Soviets' desire to obtain these items from Japan. Economic cooperation with Japan would result in two major benefits to the Soviet Union: (1) stable markets for its resources, and (2) an opportunity to obtain the advanced technology that is vital to economic growth.[15]

According to some Japanese analysts, one political objective is to prevent or obstruct the development of closer relations between Japan on the one hand and China and the United States on the other. Another political consideration the Japanese suspect is an increasing difficulty for the Soviet Union in meeting demands for oil emanating from external sources, especially Eastern Europe. If stability of supply could not be assured, Soviet influence over Eastern Europe would be weakened.[16] As these analysts see it, the Soviet leaders are haunted by the nightmare of an anti-Soviet coalition comprising Japan, the United States, and China. Japanese-Chinese normalization occurred with unanticipated speed, as did rapprochement between China and the United States. From the Soviet perspective, Japan's involvement in Siberian development would partially destroy the anti-Soviet coalition. By drawing Japan closer, the Soviet Union could move one step nearer the realization of a collective security system. It is significant, these analysts point out, that a Russian diplomat characterized Russo-Japanese cooperation in the development of Siberia as suggestive of the formation of a "Russo-Japanese Resource Alliance."[17]

It may be difficult to substantiate the argument that China figured

15 Saeki, pp. 3–4.
16 *Asahi Shimbun*, Apr. 22, 1972.
17 Ibid., May 12, 1973.

strongly in the Soviet decision to develop Siberia and the Soviet Far East. It is reasonable to assume, however, that the Soviet leaders have been acutely aware of the political and strategic implications of the development plans and Japan's role in them for Sino-Soviet relations and for Japanese relations with China.

Soviet sensitivity to Chinese views is evident. For example, shortly after the summit conference in Moscow (October 1973), Askold Biryukov, a Tass commentator, criticized China's alleged attempt to prevent rapprochement between the Soviet and the Japanese peoples:

Before and during Premier Tanaka's visit to the USSR, the Maoists and their press were literally seized [with] anti-Soviet fever. In their typical condescending manner the Peking leaders ventured to prompt the Japanese what they should and should not discuss in Moscow. They were warned not to agree on cooperation with the Soviet Union in the exploitation of Siberia's wealth, especially in the construction of a trans-Siberian oil pipeline, because this "could create a strategic problem for China."
. . . The Maoists clamped down upon the idea of building up a collective security system in Asia. They thrust upon Japan their advice not to renounce territorial claims. The Maoists still adhere to this line in their attempts to prevent the rapprochement [of] the Soviet and Japanese peoples.[18]

It is also reasonable to assume that the Soviet leaders are conscious of military implications in the development of Siberia. The development of the Tyumen oilfields and the construction of a pipeline would play an important role in supplying oil requirements for Soviet ground forces on the Sino-Soviet borders and for the Soviet Pacific Fleet. It is also reasonable to assume that the Soviet leaders are aware of the leverage they would acquire toward Japan. By being drawn economically closer, Japan might be compelled to move closer politically to insure an adequate return from the immense investment. In order to avoid Soviet interruption of supplies, Japan might have to be accommodating to Soviet wishes.

The Soviet leaders attach much importance to the *long-term* character of the economic cooperation envisaged, and they show sensitivity to political implications. As Semichastnov, first deputy minister of foreign trade, indicated, the projects are intended to be carried out over a period of fifteen to twenty years, and "the very fact they are long range will help to maintain and consolidate friendly,

18 *FBIS* (Soviet Union), Oct. 19, 1973.

good-neighbor relations between the Soviet Union and Japan."[19] The Soviet leaders are also aware of the implications of Japan's extensive involvement vis-à-vis Japanese-American relations. The close politicomilitary and economic ties between the United States and Japan have long been a source of major Soviet concern. The improved relations between the United States and the Soviet Union during the past few years somewhat diminished the urgency and intensity of Soviet concern with the United States–Japan security treaty, but a Soviet quest for its termination remains strong. The Soviet desire to reduce U.S.-Japanese politicoeconomic ties is also indicated in Soviet publications following Nixon's shocks of July and August 1971. These publications contain frequent references to the allegedly ever growing contradictions between the United States and Japan.[20]

The Soviets constantly remind the Japanese of the folly and danger of their excessive dependence on and exclusive alliance with the United States. They applaud any developments indicative of Japan's independence of the United States or Japan's pursuit of a policy at variance with that of the United States. They point out to the Japanese the availability of alternative ties with the Soviet Union. Propaganda for the expansion of trade and economic interaction has been impressive. Numerous articles have appeared since the late 1960s, especially in the past few years, emphasizing the complementarity of the economic interests of the two countries.

In view of the avid interest the Soviet Union has shown in the strained relations between the United States and Japan, it is reasonable to assume that the possible implication of Japan's extensive involvement in Siberian development has been a consideration for Soviet leaders. The deeper the extent of Japanese involvement in Siberian development, the less exclusive will be Japan's orientation toward the United States.

The Soviet Union must believe that close economic cooperation will lead to a general improvement in relations between the two countries. The following passages by Kudryavtsev, which appeared in the *Izvestia* (October 1973), are suggestive of this position:

If enormous economic relations are created and if Japan benefits from them, psychological obstacles to Japan-Soviet cooperation will be gone. . . .

[19] *Current Digest of Soviet Press*, Mar. 29, 1972, pp. 15–16.

[20] *Pravda*, Apr. 27, 1972, Aug. 4, 1973; D. Petrov, "The U.S. and Japan—A New Phase," *USA: Ekonomika, Politika, Ideologiya*, Jan. 24, 1972, in *FBIS*, Feb. 22, 1972.

. . . economic cooperation already exists between our countries. . . . But already this is insufficient; there is now talk of the joint working and exploitation of Tyumen oil, coking coal, and gas in southern Yakutia. . . . In short, the development of Soviet-Japanese relations at the present stage gives rise to the need for large-scale and long-term economic cooperation which will impart fresh scope and depth to Soviet-Japanese relations as a whole (translation from *FBIS*, Oct. 10, 1973).

Implications for the Future

It may be an exaggeration to say that the Soviet leaders expect the Northern Territories issue to disappear because of economic cooperation, but it is conceivable that they hope such cooperation will result in a quiet, de facto shelving of the issue. At minimum, the adamant intensity with which the Northern Territories issue is pressed by the Japanese might be lessened. This interpretation has some basis and is certainly consistent with the Soviet belief that the Northern Territories issue is really an artificially created one, with culpability fixed on the Japanese government. This belief is further sustained by another one, that monopoly capital and business interests in fact determine Japanese government policy and that the Siberian development projects receive solid support from Japanese economic interests.

Soviet leaders and commentators point out that Japan's need for fuel and other resources is critical, suggesting that this matter should be of vital concern to the Japanese. In contrast, they argue, the Northern Territories issue is a nonissue or a minor artificial one, propagandized by revanchists and forces who are interested in blocking the improved relations between the two countries. Russian comments have occasionally been more direct. They ask: Which is more important to Japan's national interest, the Northern Territories or access to fuel and other resources?

What considerations have shaped Japan's attitude and its cooperation in the Siberian development project? Japan's attitude has been very cautious, because Japan is well aware that its involvement is potentially advantageous, as well as potentially dangerous, from the standpoint of both economics and foreign security policy.

The Japanese economy depends heavily on imports of fuel and raw materials, and the Japanese are acutely aware that they must ensure a steady influx of these materials. Source diversification is desired in order to assure supply in view of the growing competition among the industrial nations and to avoid excessive dependence on any one source, reducing the harmful effect on the Japanese economy in the event of a supply interruption. Japan imports 99 percent of all the oil it consumes, and, given its low inventory capacity and ever increasing need, the Japanese economy would be seriously damaged within a short time if the flow of oil were interrupted. Thus, stability of supply is a primary goal—stability that is relatively immune from the vicissitudes of international politics and the international supply situation.[21] The Tyumen project would guarantee delivery of crude oil for twenty years—in other words, a long-term supply. Moreover, the oil would have a low sulphur content.[22]

As seen by the Japanese, their economy requires an expansion of export trade to sustain a high growth rate and to maintain a favorable balance of payments. They have duly noted the growth in the volume of Soviet foreign trade with nonsocialist countries and regard the Siberian development projects as providing a good opportunity to acquire access to the Soviet market.[23] Under the Tyumen project Japan would deliver pipes, equipment, and consumer goods, and the amount of trade turnover would be greatly increased. Japanese-Soviet trade has been on the increase, and, for the year 1973, trade between the two countries amounted to $1,562 million. Japanese exports came to $484 million, while imports totaled $1,078 million. In a February 1974 meeting, Soviet and Japanese trade officials agreed to further expand bilateral trade. In 1974, total Japanese exports to the Soviet Union are expected to increase 50 percent over the total for 1973. This increase will center on machinery, iron and steel products, chemical goods, textiles, and textile products.[24]

In addition to economic considerations, the Japanese leaders are conscious of the political implications of closer economic cooperation with the Soviet Union. They feel that Japan would obtain leverage vis-à-vis the Soviet Union, China, and the United States. Japan's cooperation would provide leverage against the Soviet Union[25] on political questions, possibly including the Northern Territories issue. The improved relations accompanying massive economic entanglement might provide more opportunity for possible resolution of the matter.

[21] Saeki, pp. 4–5.
[22] *Nihon Keizai Shimbun*, Feb. 24, 1972.
[23] Saeki, p. 4.
[24] *FBIS*, Feb. 25, 1974.
[25] *Nihon Keizai Shimbun*, Feb. 22, 1972.

The Japanese are also conscious of the effect Japanese-Soviet economic cooperation would have on China. The Japanese government's
serious move toward the Siberian development projects came after
the Japan-China normalization. The Japanese leaders sensed enormous Soviet distrust and a suspicion that Japanese-Chinese collusion
against the Soviet Union might be taking place. Having normalized
relations with China, they felt a need to maintain a balance by
improving relations with the Soviet Union. This was perhaps compounded by a decline of Premier Tanaka's popularity in Japan;
and Japanese-Soviet relations provided a potentially meaningful
issue to demonstrate the legitimacy of his leadership. A movement
toward the Soviet Union in the economic sphere would also serve
as a countervailing force vis-à-vis the United States. Japanese leaders
have been sensitive to Chinese views on Japanese-Soviet economic
cooperation.[26] The Chinese have on numerous occasions expressed
their concern with the Tyumen project in particular. In January
1973 Chou En-lai told Nakasone, the Japanese minister of international trade and industry, of the risks in relying on the Soviet Union
for resource supply, saying the Chinese know better than anyone
that the Russians are not to be trusted. He said that he was opposed
to the Tyumen project as it would strengthen the Soviet armed
forces in the Far East.

Aside from strategic implications, China may also be concerned
with the long-term implications of the development of an economic
infrastructure near its Siberian borders. Japan's position in this
respect is that energy sources are critical enough to justify diversification efforts. Of course, the Japanese themselves are concerned with
the prospect that Soviet military capability would be strengthened
by the development of the Tyumen.[27] At the same time the Japanese
are aware that Japan's massive involvement in the Siberian projects
would make Japan vulnerable to Soviet pressure.[28] Japan might be
compelled to take the Soviet side against China or the United States,
if only to protect investments and to assure a continued flow of oil
and raw materials. The Japanese are concerned about the possibility
that the Soviet Union might interrupt supplies or otherwise use
Japan's involvement in the Tyumen project as political leverage,
eventually weakening Japan's political position. Japan's desire to

[26] Ibid., Mar. 1, July 26, 1973.
[27] Ibid., Jan. 21, 1972.
[28] Ibid., Mar. 1, 1973.

see the United States become involved is designed as insurance against possible noncompliance on the part of the Soviet Union.[29] While the Japanese government has accepted the Soviet Union as a source of energy supply, it does not want to depend on the Soviet Union for more than 10 percent of its oil imports.[30] A major escalation of the Sino-Soviet conflict might delay the project and result in the destruction of the facilities. Japan in this case would not have a stable supply and could even lose its capital investments. In any case, present Soviet terms are unsatisfactory to Japan, especially with regard to the amount of oil supplied.

Another major factor shaping the Japanese government's posture toward the Siberian development projects is the positive attitude among those in Japanese industrial and business circles toward these projects. The highly interdependent relationship between government leaders and these interests in Japan make the former highly susceptible to the preferences of the latter. The enthusiasm of business leaders for the Siberian projects is well known and has been conveyed to the political leaders. For example, a business leader (Nagano) called upon Foreign Minister Ohira to practice separation of economic and political issues, urging Ohira not to use the Siberian issue as leverage for the Northern Territories issue. The desire for early resolution of the development issue on the part of those in business circles is a factor that political leaders cannot ignore. This is not to deny that the Japanese government has provided close "guidance" on behalf of the business interests throughout the negotiations on the Siberian project issue. There has been a close working relationship, and the government leadership on the whole has served as a sobering and cautious influence.

A major impetus to the improvement in Soviet-Japanese relations has come from evolving relations between the United States and China, and between Japan and China. They have been further facilitated by the show of flexibility on the part of Tanaka and Ohira, indicating that Japan would be prepared to pursue the question of participation in Siberian economic development projects as distinct from progress on the Northern Territories issue. For the Soviets, this was a welcome development, signifying that Japan might be willing to shelve the question of the territories altogether. It even

[29] *Asahi Shimbun*, May 28, June 17, 1972.

[30] Raymond Albright, "Siberian Energy for Japan and the United States" (Paper delivered at the Fifteenth Session, Senior Seminar in Foreign Policy, Dept. of State, 1972–73), pp. 3–18.

led to speculation among some Soviets that a peace treaty might be forthcoming, one based on the Soviet stand.[31] As it turned out, the summit talks of October 1973 amply demonstrated the inseparability and interaction of the political and economic issues.

Summary and Interpretation

Noneconomic considerations consistently and significantly shaped the nature of bilateral relations even though there was congruence in economic objectives. A set of political factors provided the first opportunities for exploration and consummation of the measures of economic cooperation attained in the late 1960s. These factors included (1) the reduction of enmity between the United States and the Soviet Union, (2) the presence of the Sino-Soviet conflict, and (3) Japan's growing power, relative to the United States.

Soviet economic requirements as well as Soviet zeal for the development of Siberia became evident after the announcement of the Five-Year Plan. Collaterally, Japan's growing need for fuel resources and raw materials became increasingly apparent. Without these complementary economic requirements, developments leading to the 1973 summit meeting—especially the kinds of talks held on the Northern Territories issue—might not have occurred. The Soviet Union probably would have been less agreeable to discussions on the Northern Territories issue, and Japan might not have taken the position it did on the political and economic questions.

It must also be recognized that the following political factors have been critical in facilitating and constraining Soviet-Japanese relations in recent years. (1) The evolving American-Chinese relations since July 1971 gave Japan greater latitude in foreign policy choices and provided less constraint on closer economic cooperation with the Soviet Union. The Soviets recognized the opportunity to loosen American-Japanese ties and to draw closer to Japan. The American-Chinese demarche provided an incentive for both the Soviet Union and Japan to cooperate in their relations with the United States. (2) The continued Sino-Soviet conflict provided an incentive to the Soviet Union to move closer to and solidify its relations with Japan. The Soviet Union has an interest in forestalling closer relations between Japan and China. Having achieved normal-

[31] Indeed, during my visit to the Soviet Union in the summer of 1973, one Soviet expert indicated optimism in this regard, saying that a peace treaty would be signed soon.

ization with China, Japan, too, felt it prudent to improve relations with the Soviet Union. Both the Soviet Union and Japan were aware that these closer relations would provide them leverage against China. The political objectives heightened interest in, and gave impetus to, economic cooperation, with each side mindful of the political implications, as well as the economic benefits to be accrued. Despite complementary economic interests, it is the political and security considerations that have prevented a complete normalization and have restrained the tempo and extent of economic cooperation between the two countries.

Case 2: The Oil Crisis

At its October 17, 1973, meeting, the Organization of Arab Petroleum Exporting Countries (OAPEC) decided to cut oil production by 5 to 10 percent. The move was designed to build up pressure for a Middle Eastern settlement by causing energy shortages in Western Europe and Japan. On November 5, OAPEC announced a 25-percent reduction in production based on the September output and a further 5-percent cut beginning in December. OAPEC stipulated that these further reductions should not hurt countries friendly to the Arab countries cause.[32]

On November 6, the Middle East Economic Survey reported that Saudi Arabia had advised Japan it must sever diplomatic and economic ties with Israel if it hoped to gain favored status with Saudi Arabia and other Arab oil suppliers.[33] This report was confirmed on November 19, when Saudi Arabia's petroleum minister, Sheikh Ahmed Zaki Yamani, said that Japan must break relations with Israel or otherwise assist Arab nations in a significant manner to qualify for exemption from Arab oil cutbacks.[34]

The Japanese government responded by abandoning its neutral stand on the Middle East conflict and coming out in stronger support of the Arab position. Thus, on November 22, the chief cabinet secretary, Nikaido, issued a statement urging Israel to withdraw from territories occupied during the 1967 war, warning that "depending on future developments," the Japanese government "may

[32] *Japan Times,* Nov. 5, 6, 1973.
[33] Ibid., Nov. 8, 1973.
[34] Ibid., Nov. 20, 1973.

have to reconsider its policy toward Israel." With oil accounting for practically all of Japan's energy requirements, and 40 percent of its supply coming from the Arab states, there is no doubt that a critical need for oil was the decisive reason for this policy shift.

The shift, however, did not entirely satisfy the Arabs. Preceding the OAPEC announcement on December 9 of a new 5-perecent cut in oil production beginning January 1, there was a warning from Yamani that the January decrease would apply to Japan, even though it had been exempted from the December supply cut.[35]

In response, Tanaka met with two Arab ministers on December 10; he stated that Japan would strengthen its ties with Arabs in diplomatic and economic fields, and pledged an expansion in economic assistance.[36] On the same day, Deputy Premier Miki left Tokyo on a three-week tour of the Middle East, a tour described by Tanaka as designed "to promote friendship and good neighborly relations between Japan and the Arab nations." In Miki's words, the trip was made "to find ways in which Japan could contribute to a settlement of the Middle East conflict."[37] Despite the official explanations, it is clear that Miki's mission was to clarify Japan's November 22 statement regarding the Middle East and discuss ways in which Japan might help the Arab nations in economic and technical fields. It was reported that Miki's offers included Japanese assistance in the Suez Canal dredging project and oil refinery construction.[38]

On December 25, OAPEC announced that, effective January, it would lower the production cut from 25 to 15 percent of the September level.[39] The additional 5-percent cutback announced for January was also bypassed. That Japan was finally being considered a friendly country was welcome news. However, it was tempered by the announcement that Persian Gulf states had two days earlier decided to double the price of oil[40] and, even more significant, the fear that Japan would be placed on constant call for displays of "friendship" to stay on the friendly list. Furthermore, given the working of the system under which major international oil companies control the distribution of 80 percent of the Arabian oil,

[35] Ibid., Dec. 6, 1973.
[36] Ibid., Dec. 10, 11, 1973.
[37] Ibid.
[38] Ibid., Dec. 18, 1973.
[39] Ibid., Dec. 26, 1973.
[40] Ibid., Dec. 24, 1973.

the Japanese had no absolute guarantee that Japan's actual needs would be fully supplied. Japan imports 61.2 percent of its oil imports through major international companies such as Exxon.

As might have been expected, the oil crisis has had an adverse impact on Japan's relations with the United States, by reinforcing mutual suspicions. Japanese resentment toward the United States, and Secretary of State Kissinger in particular, has been reinforced by Kissinger's alleged attitude of indifference toward the Japanese predicament, as shown during his brief stopover in Tokyo in November 1973.[41] The depth of Japanese suspicions in some circles is indicated by an interpretation that the oil crisis was an outcome of a Kissinger conspiracy designed to cripple the Japanese economy. This view was expressed publicly in the leading paper *Asahi* and appears to be shared even by some members of the Liberal Democratic party.

The Japanese decision to change its stand toward the Arabs was made in full awareness that such a policy would be at variance with the express U.S. position; and the November 22 policy announcement and pro forma notification of the United States was greeted in the United States with an official expression of regret. While appreciating Japan's predicament, U.S. policymakers appeared to have perceived Japan's policy shift as indicative of a trend toward greater divergence of U.S. and Japanese policies. From the perspectives of both countries, the oil crisis has heightened tension, sensitizing each side to the growing possibility of conflicting policy goals, and further narrowing the area of meaningful consultation or coordination.

Japan's critical dependence on oil supplies, highlighted dramatically during the 1973–74 crisis, has intensified its need to find diversified sources of energy supplies. This imperative may be expected to condition to some extent Japan's relations with the Soviet Union and the People's Republic of China. There will be a greater incentive for Japan to improve its relations with both these countries to assure itself access to oil and other energy resources. On the other hand, the respective policies of the Soviet Union and China toward Japan may be influenced by Soviet and Chinese perceptions of Japan's economic vulnerability and its critical need for energy supplies.

The oil crisis also affected the content of Japan's defense policy. On December 22, 1973, the Japan Defense Agency (JDA) announced a reduction in its defense request for the year 1974–75 by approximately 8 billion yen. This meant, among other things, that the order

41 Ibid., Nov. 21, 1973.

for acquisition of key equipment was to be delayed. The self-imposed reduction was explained as a measure taken in compliance with the general directive for reducing aggregative demand. The content of the Fourth Defense Plan might not be altered, but the implementation of the plan would be delayed beyond the time frame originally envisaged. Once such a reduction is made without creating an evident adverse impact on Japan's security, the JDA may find it difficult to convince skeptics that the original defense plan was justified, even if the economic situation improves.

The New Europe
A Unified Bloc or Blocked Unity?

Edward L. Morse

THE psychological atmosphere in Europe during the winter of
1973–74 posed a striking contrast to the euphoria of the previous
year. While the summit conference of heads of government of European Community (EC) countries in mid-December 1973 proclaimed
the unfolding of a new European identity, the statement was more
fundamentally a cosmetic attempt to disguise underlying foreign
policy disagreements and severe domestic political crises in each of
the countries.[1] The superficial nature of the Copenhagen proclamation was soon highlighted as the British government, confronting an
intractable coal miners' strike and eventual elections, as well as an
electorate for which membership in the European Community had
not been popular, refused to compromise its demands for implementing an EC regional fund from which it would benefit. This led to a
failure to agree on a regional funding formula by the January 1,
1974, deadline. Within the following three weeks the French government provoked its EC partners by striking a bilateral trade deal
with Saudi Arabia, assuring the French a secure supply of high-
priced crude oil in return for almost $1 billion in armaments, and
thereby undermining any European attempt to formulate a common
policy in energy. That same French government, on January 18, 1974,
"temporarily" withdrew from the common float of EC currencies,
thus relinquishing a policy for which it had previously been the
major spokesman and which had been one of the major symbols of
EC unity.

In January 1974, British elections held in response to the coal
miners' strike resulted in a minority Labour government, under
Harold Wilson, which actively urged a renegotiation of the terms
of British membership in the European Community and which was
more visibly "Atlanticist" in its underlying attitudes. At the same

---

[1] The EC declaration on the nature of the "European Identity" can be found
in *Survival* 16, no. 2 (Mar.–Apr. 1974): 92–93.

time, the French government, for complex political factors associated with the failing health of President Georges Pompidou and the increasing loss of popular support for the majority Gaullist coalition, readopted a Gaullian policy of autonomy and a foreign policy of independence. This made it extremely difficult for other EC governments to achieve compromise with the British or French governments on regional, agricultural, energy, or foreign policy (especially toward the United States and the Middle East). This difficulty was compounded by domestic political problems in Germany, whose government, faced with dissent within the ruling Socialist–Free Democrat coalition over major domestic legislation, was less and less willing to fund Common Market projects like the Common Agricultural Policy (CAP) and the new regional fund.

By the winter of 1973–74, in short, there was no clear pattern of political compromise among West European governments and little apparent willingness in any of the major governments to continue the "relaunching" of Europe begun in 1969 or to implement their earlier proclamation of a new European identity.[2] This contrasts markedly with the situation in Europe the previous winter. In October 1972 a much heralded summit of EC governments held in Paris committed each of the members to continue the process of monetary and economic unification, general policy coordination in domestic and foreign affairs, and eventual political integration. Despite what has been characterized as an underlying malaise in Europe,[3] by January 1, 1973, with the formal accession of Britain, Denmark, and Ireland to the European Community, it appeared that the momentum for European unity that had begun in the context of the summit at The Hague in December 1969 would continue to mount, especially, if not only, because the European governments each had a domestic political stake in the success of the Common Market.[4] Yet one year later the major characteristics of European politics were disunion rather than unification, independent national

[2] See the argument of Walter Lacqueur, "The Idea of Europe Runs Out of Gas," *New York Times Magazine*, Jan. 20, 1974, pp. 12 ff.

[3] This argument is summarized in Alfred Grosser, "Europe: Community of Malaise," *Foreign Policy*, no. 15 (Summer 1974), pp. 169–82.

[4] The communiqué of the October 1972 summit meeting is reproduced in *Survival* 15, no. 1 (Jan.–Feb. 1973): 27–30. An optimistic analysis of European prospects in mid-1973 by a leading European journalist may be found in Theo Sommer, "The Community Is Working," *Foreign Affairs* 51, no. 3 (July 1973): 747–60.

actions as opposed to the coordination of common policies, and a generalized pessimism about the viability of the European Community in contrast to the exuberant optimism of 1972–73.

It is by no means clear why this dramatic change occurred in Europe over such a short period of time. While theorists of the integration process have recently taken into account conditions that might lead to "spillback" rather than "spillover" during the integration process,[5] the basic factors that motivated economic integration in Europe were still prominent in 1974, and "spillback" alone could not explain the course of events. In particular, the level of economic interdependence among the European societies—as measured by the growth of the external sector in each of the economies and their increased orientation to intra-European trade—has become so great that the cost of reasserting economic autonomy remains prohibitive in terms of welfare losses that would result as well as in psychological terms (given restricted national horizons). Nor is it clear that another revival in the European movement will not occur in the near future.

If a revival and relative stagnation in Europeanism are major alternatives to the EC members, what factors are likely to lead to one and what factors to the other? What factors were responsible for the breakdown in the EC revival in 1973–74? How do these factors relate to the revival that had begun in 1969–70? The answers to the last two questions are critical for a response to the first, and any attempt to come to grips with them must take into account other recent and dramatic changes in the international system, as well as the nature of political compromise within Europe. This essay will turn first to those other changes and then to the nature of political decision-making within the European Community. Finally, it will return to the question of Europe's future and make a modest effort at prediction.

Europe and the International Upheaval

If the immediate causes of the radical shift in the European movement in the 1970s are somewhat obscure, it is evident that changes in Europe are related to other recent shifts in the international system. They are most obviously related to the 1973 Yom Kippur War

[5] The phenomenon of "spillback" is explained in Leon N. Lindberg and Stuart A. Scheingold, *Europe's Would-be Polity* (Englewood Cliffs, N.J.: Prentice-Hall, 1970), chap. 6.

in the Middle East. That war itself reflected the growing confidence of the Arab oil-exporting countries, whose governments have been able to take advantage of their oligopolistic position in the energy market and assert economic power that appears wholly incommensurate with the size of their populations and their technological base. The sense of European powerlessness in securing oil resources, which are fundamental to the economic and social stability of all highly industrialized societies, was the immediate provocation of the recent crisis in Europe. By quadrupling the price of crude oil in a period of less than six months, the Arab oil-exporting countries effectively disrupted fundamental calculations of relative power and of risks and stakes involved in European policy toward the Middle East.

This change itself followed other basic changes in the general international setting in the 1970s. The devaluation of the dollar in 1971 and the subsequent movement toward a generalized regime of floating exchange rates disrupted the basic rules of the game of international monetary affairs that had been established in the post World War II period. The shift from a world of fixed rates of exchange to one of floating currencies had been seen, between 1971 and 1973, in part as a result of an inevitable secular decline in American economic power and a devolution of that power to Europe, Japan, and the Soviet Union.[6] Indeed, that decline in America's relative power seemed to be so universally recognized that Richard Nixon, in an interview with *Time* in early 1972, argued that a new five-power world was emerging, which could be viewed as both pluralistic and stable.[7]

By the winter of 1973–74, however, predictions concerning the secular decline in American economic and military power seemed far more tenuous.[8] In the aftermath of the energy crisis, it was recognized that the relative invulnerability of the U.S. economy to blackmail by the governments of supplier countries had great consequences for predictions of America's relative power. In a newly emerging era, when security of supply of raw materials, it seemed, was rivaling economic growth as the major motivation of foreign economic policy, relative economic power might no longer be seen

[6] Harold van Buren Cleveland, "How the Dollar Standard Died," *Foreign Policy*, no. 5 (Winter 1971–72), pp. 41–51.

[7] Jan. 3, 1972, p. 15.

[8] See Paul Lewis, "Dollar Resumes Its Global Ascendancy," *Financial Times*, Apr. 29, 1974, p. 15.

primarily as a reflection of the growth of a country's GNP and the amount of its international trade. Both, after all, might well stagnate relative to their levels in the 1950s and 1960s. Rather the government of the most self-sufficient economy, whose sources of supply of energy and other raw materials were largely internal, was likely to gain relative to the others. Thus, the relatively self-sufficient United States, far less vulnerable than either Japan or Western Europe, would perhaps reverse America's secular economic decline and assure continued American predominance in the international system.

It is obvious that the recalculation of American power in the aftermath of the energy crisis of 1973–74 had significant effects on the European mood and the prognosis for the European challenge to the United States in international affairs. These effects were reflected in the notion of what that European challenge might consist. The French political analyst Pierre Hassner, writing in early 1973, described the basis of the new Europe.[9] Hassner assumed: (1) that Europe was not militarily united and was not likely to be in the near future, given the economic and political costs of military investment in an era of costly technology, détente, and popular pacifism; (2) that the nuclear stalemate between the superpowers had, at any rate, rendered military force less useful and relevant to political goals; and (3) that economic diplomacy was now becoming more important than ever. In such a system, the European Community, representing the largest trading bloc in the world, could be expected to provide a new model of international relations. If the American economist Richard N. Cooper was correct in arguing that foreign economic policy is now the basis for foreign policy in general,[10] then the European Community offered a new model of "civilized international politics" in a world where military power might well be irrelevant for most and where economic relations would largely concern the wealthy, industrialized societies.

The model of the new type of foreign policy, implemented by the European Community and fostering continued EC economic advance, was not visibly appropriate to the world of 1974. Rather than orienting the bases of foreign economic policy toward the United

[9] *Europe in the Age of Negotiation,* Washington Papers, no. 8 (Washington, D.C.: Center for Strategic and International Studies, Georgetown University, 1973).

[10] "Trade Policy Is Foreign Policy," *Foreign Policy,* no. 9 (Winter 1972–73), pp. 18–36.

States and other areas of the industrialized world under the assumptions of continued and uninterrupted growth in trade in industrial products and consumer goods, the EC governments would have to focus more narrowly on the security of sources of supply of major raw materials from less developed societies, and especially from the Middle East. Several general implications of this shift are worth noting. The expected orientation of foreign economic policy toward North America and Japan implied the need to maintain some universal framework like the General Agreement on Tariffs and Trade (GATT) for appropriate multilateral negotiations. The new focus on security of supply and toward the Middle East governments of oil-exporting societies was more likely to result in bilateral negotiations. Whereas the emphasis on industrialized area trade reflected a concern with sharing an increasingly large and interdependent network of relationships, the newer emphasis reflected a concern with maintaining relative invulnerability in terms of access of supply in a set of overlapping and bilateral (rather than multilateral and interdependent) relations.

The new orientation in European foreign economic policy created additional challenges. The Middle East had in fact always been of concern to an incipient and common European foreign policy. Ideally, the Europeans have hoped to be able to develop a situation in which they would be unified as well as free of the impediments of Soviet and American "hegemony." Should Europe gain equality with the superpowers, it would, as a new economic superpower, be freer to pursue its own "mission" in the world.[11] Basic to that mission has been the notion that Europe has a natural sphere of influence toward which it should orient a special policy. Included in this sphere are the Mediterranean Sea, North Africa, the former African colonial areas, and the Middle East.[12] This notion has been rationalized in terms of the historical relationships between Europe and these areas. Noteworthy in these relationships, of course, is continued European predominance. Thus, while the need to deal with Arab oil-exporting governments on a special basis is not new, the reversal of expected roles that took place in 1973 has been shocking to the notion of this European mission. As a result, the likelihood of implementing that mission in the future is now extremely low.

[11] See Johan Galtung, *The European Community: A Superpower in the Making* (London: George Allen and Unwin, 1973).

[12] See Richard Bailey, *The European Community in the World* (London: Midway, 1973).

There is an additional irony in the relationship between the EC governments and those of the Middle East. In confronting the Soviet Union at the height of the cold war or even in the Conference on Security and Cooperation in Europe (after July 1973), just as in confronting the United States during the Kennedy Round in the GATT or in monetary affairs after 1971, the EC governments had an incentive to act in unity. Yet in confronting their former protectorates and colonies in the Middle East, these same governments were unable to act in harmony and began, through independent initiatives, to compete with one another for secure oil supplies.

It is questionable whether the energy crisis of the winter of 1973–74 triggered a chain of events that fragmented the European Community and that reflected an already existing underlying malaise in Europe, or whether it represented a new stress on the Community, a stress symbolizing a new factor of international politics and one that will also characterize the international arena for the foreseeable future. The former view would argue that the Community governments had already taken all feasible political initiatives in their creation of a customs union and the Common Agricultural Policy. Any additional decision on social affairs, monetary policy, harmonization of tax policy, etc., would pose a major dilemma for each government insofar as it would require what no decision had hitherto made necessary: the relinquishing of sovereign rights.[13] The latter view would argue that the energy crisis and the reaction of the various European governments to it reflect a new urgency in dealing with security of supply of raw materials and other resources. Concern for security of supply simply to maintain an existing lifestyle and level of consumption may well become a goal of equal priority to—if not greater priority than—economic growth for all industrialized societies in the near future. Whereas economic growth, as a major governmental priority, led naturally to multilateral cooperation of the sort once represented in the European Community, security of supply leads more naturally to bilateral relations with suppliers and a competition among industrialized societies, which is clearly not conducive to cooperative behavior.

Both of these views are important in understanding the recent fragmentation in Europe, but they are not sufficient explanations. Of additional importance are the nature of bargains that may be

13 This is the argument of John Pinder, "Positive Integration or Negative Integration: Some Problems of Economic Union in the EEC," *The World Today* 24 (Jan. 1968):88–110.

struck within Europe between the major governments, and the domestic political concerns of each government. It will be argued below
that European cooperation has been possible when the major governments have been able to pursue a set of compatible but divergent
goals. When they pursue similar goals, political bargains among them
are less feasible, and political conflict more likely.[14] This paradox
results from the likelihood that in pursuing similar goals, the European governments will find that they all cannot achieve them simultaneously and that one government's gain will be another's loss.
Thus Britain, France, and Germany cannot each achieve leadership
in the Community simultaneously, if leadership is the objective of
each. But if each is pursuing a set of different but compatible goals,
mutual agreements are more likely to result.

It will be argued below that the consensus achieved in the Community in the period 1969–73 resulted from a set of mutually reinforcing political compromises achieved by the major European governments, allowing them each to find in Europeanism not simply a
set of compatible foreign policy objectives but domestic policy pay-
offs as well. The fragmentation in Europe that occurred after 1973
can also be largely explained by these two factors. On the one hand,
the European governments were no longer as able to trade off their
mutually reinforcing goals as they had been in the earlier period.
On the other hand, none of the major European governments found
in institutionalizing the mechanisms of the European Community
the sort of domestic political gains that it had found earlier. The
inevitable result is disunity.

The European Revival of 1969

The revival of the European movement after 1969 was no more apparent than at the summit held at The Hague in December of that
year.[15] This political meeting set the tone for European politics for
the next three years and launched a wave of exuberance and optimism
for European political integration. The heads of government of the
six EC members committed themselves to three apparently momen-

14 For an alternative view, see Stanley Hoffmann, "Toward a Common European
Foreign Policy?" in *The United States and Western Europe*, ed. Wolfram Hanrieder (Cambridge, Mass.: Winthrop, 1974), pp. 79–105.

15 See Roger Morgan, *West European Politics since 1945: The Shaping of the
European Community* (London: B. T. Batsford, 1972), pp. 209–26.

tous decisions at The Hague. First, they decided to begin negotiations for opening the three European organizations—the European Economic Community, Euratom, and the Coal and Steel Community—to those members of the European Free Trade Association (EFTA) whose governments wished to join. This meant an invitation, in particular, to the United Kingdom, which had thrice in the previous decade appealed to these organizations for membership and had each time confronted de Gaulle's veto. Second, the summit meeting committed the member governments to begin feasibility studies concerning the formation of a monetary union in Europe to complement the common policies that had already been created. Third, the members agreed to harmonize their foreign policies in those areas where such policy coordination was feasible and desirable.

Each of these three decisions was of momentous importance. The decision to begin negotiations for enlarging the Common Market was viewed as an effort to revive the European movement, which had stagnated by the end of the 1960s, in part as a result of de Gaulle's refusal to permit European institutions to develop further. With British accession to Europe, a more widely based set of European institutions could grow; and the very act of negotiating entry would commit the members to transcend the stagnation in the development of European political institutions. The decision to begin studies for monetary union was of even greater political importance. By that decision—and by the eventual acceptance of a common monetary policy—the member governments were apparently committing themselves to give up precious sovereign rights, thus representing their own long-term goal for creating a unified political entity in Europe. The third decision, the coordination of foreign policies, was the capstone of the commitment to political unification, as it represented the desirability of creating a European identity in the international arena that would allow Europe eventually to compete with China, the United States, and Russia for global stakes.

The decisions made at The Hague in 1969 represent a dramatic change in the political climate in Europe. Just a little more than a year before that meeting, de Gaulle had once more vetoed an effort by Britain to join the Common Market, and no new policy initiatives had been made in Europe since the commitment to implement the Common Agricultural Policy in 1964. Europe seemed to be at a dead-end in terms of policy innovation and national commitments, and a revival of the climate of the late 1950s seemed unlikely. Yet such a revival is exactly what occurred. The most obvious reason for this turn of events has to do with the fact that in 1969 new leadership appeared in both Germany and France. Since Franco-German agreements have been the requisite of any European initiative since the formation of the Coal and Steel Community in the early 1950s, the commitment of new governments in each to Europe in 1969 lay at the heart of the summit's policy success.

Charles de Gaulle resigned in April 1969 when his proposals concerning regional reform in France failed to be ratified in a national referendum. The new government, under President Georges Pompidou, was elected shortly thereafter. Pompidou's about-face on the French position toward Europe stemmed from a series of factors, some of which relate to differences between himself and de Gaulle as political leaders, and others of which were contextual.[16]

Pompidou clearly could not rely on the sort of legitimacy that de Gaulle had created around his "historical personality." Having entered politics as a technocrat in de Gaulle's personal entourage rather than through a series of heroic acts (like de Gaulle's leadership in the liberation of France during World War II, his having rescued the French political system from civil war during the Algerian conflict, and his having written the Constitution of the Fifth Republic), Pompidou had to be more circumspect in his strategic policy choices.[17] De Gaulle had created a series of great undertakings in French foreign policy, which revolved around his quest for French autonomy and grandeur, and which was based on his own special historical relationship with the French electorate. Pompidou had to be far more pragmatic in selecting policy choices. He saw in a decision to focus on European integration a dual personal political gain. On the one hand, Europeanism had always been popular in France in spite of de Gaulle's challenges to its viability. By leading Europe in a political revival, Pompidou hoped to earn domestic political support that he felt was lacking after his closely contested presidential election. With enhanced domestic support he would be better able to pursue a variety of domestic and foreign policy programs. On the other hand, by choosing the popular issue of

16 For a discussion of continuity and change in French foreign policy in the 1960s and early 1970s, see Edward Kolodziej, *French International Policy under de Gaulle and Pompidou: The Politics of Grandeur* (Ithaca, N.Y.: Cornell University Press, 1974).

17 See Stanley Hoffmann, "Heroic Leadership: The Case of Modern France," in *Political Leadership in Industrialized Societies*, ed. Lewis J. Edinger (New York: John Wiley, 1967), pp. 108–54.

Europe, Pompidou also apparently felt that he could free himself
of some of the constraints imposed on him by right-wing Gaullists
upon whom he had to rely for political support. If he was able to
build a sufficiently large political base, he would be able to circum-
vent the impediments placed before him by right-wing Gaullists like
Michel Debré and Pierre Messmer.

The contextual changes in French politics in 1969 are as important in understanding Pompidou's turn toward Europe as is the
change in political leadership. These contextual factors were so
fundamental that they might well have turned de Gaulle's attention
toward European integration had he remained in office.[18] France in
1969 was a far weaker state than it had been in 1967–68. The policy
of independence, which had been based on a strong leadership,
buoyant balance-of-payments surpluses, curtailed domestic consumption, and a high priority for defense-related expenditures, could no
longer be implemented after the events of May 1968. The worker-
student strikes in France were of tremendous cost to the earlier
French policy. The wage settlement that had brought the strikes to
a close were highly inflationary for the French economy and had
resulted in a severely weakened French franc (devalued in August
1969) and stringent price controls and curtailment of governmental
expenditures. In short, the settlement was of devastating consequence
for the domestic support of the policy of independence.

The devaluation of the French franc in mid-1969, coupled with the
revaluation of the German mark a few weeks later, also had consequences for France's earlier European policy. That policy had been
based on a trade-off between French and German interests in
Europe.[19] The customs union, created in Europe in 1968, was viewed
as a primary benefit for Germany, and was expected to facilitate the
expansion of German industrial exports in Europe. The Common
Agricultural Policy, implemented in complementary stages, was
viewed as France's primary gain from the Common Market, since
France possessed the most fertile and productive farmlands in Europe.
But the CAP was itself dependent on a series of difficult compromises
over targeted prices for each agricultural commodity, and these compromises depended on the maintenance of virtually fixed exchange
rates in Europe. Once the franc depreciated and the mark appre-

---

[18] I argued this case in greater detail in *Foreign Policy and Interdependence
in Gaullist France* (Princeton: Princeton University Press, 1973).

[19] See Leon Lindberg, "Decision-making and Integration in the European
Community," *International Organization* 29, no. 1 (Winter 1965):56–80.

ciated, the Common Agricultural Policy was difficult to implement. Thus, the realization that parities could be changed was a fundamental inducement to the French government to create a monetary union in Europe—less in order to integrate Europe politically than as a means of preserving fixed exchange rates and thereby preserving CAP, France's major gain from Europe.[20]

An additional consequence of the events of May 1968 for the French government was the realization that the political legitimacy not only of the French government but also of the institutions of the political system of the Fifth Republic was open to question. The fear that those events would recur in an even more severe form haunted the government of Georges Pompidou throughout his four-and-one-half year term as president. The movement toward Europe, which would benefit French consumers and perhaps pacify opponents of the regime, would, it was hoped, bolster the regime's legitimacy, just as it would help preserve the CAP and perhaps also marshal a wider range of support to maintain the franc's new parity.

The reversal of the French government's attitude toward British membership in the Common Market was also part of this general change in the context of French policy. Severely weakened economically by the aftermath of the events of May, the French government feared that the strong German economy would eventually dominate Europe. It perhaps also began to realize that the long-term coincidence of German and French objectives in Europe, upon which de Gaulle had based his European policy, would fail to materialize. Germany would be tied to American policy in Europe far more than any other European government would as a result of Germany's critical security problem as a denuclearized power bordering the Soviet bloc. Britain, rather than Germany, shared the French government's long-term goal of an autonomous Europe, free from the dominance of any superpower. Moreover, it was now realized that Britain's membership in the Common Market would pose a convenient economic counterweight with France to German economic dominance in Europe. For all of these reasons, the French government not only was in favor of reviving the European movement but also vigorously supported British membership.

The German coalition government, composed of the Socialist and Free Democrat parties and under the leadership of Socialist Chancellor Willy Brandt, was another new actor in Europe in the fall of

[20] See Edward L. Morse, "European Monetary Union and American Foreign Economic Policy," in Hanrieder, pp. 187–210.

1969. It, like the new government in France, was committed to a revival of European political institutions and, like France, for reasons that had to do with other political objectives. The new German government was elected primarily on the basis of a foreign policy program and, because of the weakness of the legislative coalition upon which it was based, realized that it would be unable to implement any elements of the traditional domestic Socialist program lest Free Democrat party support be withdrawn. The new foreign policy program was oriented toward the acceptance of the territorial status quo in Eastern Europe.[21] The *Ostpolitik* of the new government had reversed the traditional German objectives toward Eastern Europe. Traditionally, the conservative German government had argued that through a policy of strength (via alliance in NATO and European integration), it would be able to negotiate successfully German reunification, and that after reunification was achieved an era of détente in Europe would become feasible. The new government, banking on the support of a new generation in German society and the failure of the older Christian Democratic Union Eastern policies, reversed the traditional formula for reunification. Détente now would be the first step, and it would involve recognition of the borders imposed on Europe after World War II, establishment of economic ties between Germany and all of the Eastern bloc societies, and recognition of the existence of East Germany.

The new German policy toward Eastern Europe inevitably raised suspicions in other Western governments concerning Germany's reliability as a security and economic partner. The successful pursuit of *Ostpolitik* therefore required the pacification of Western fears lest such suspicions eliminate Western support for Germany's foreign policy. The successful conclusion of *Ostpolitik* also virtually required the German government to endorse new initiatives to reinforce either NATO or the European Community, and made Brandt as avid an advocate of Europeanism as was Pompidou at the summit held at The Hague.

Even had Germany not required Western support for its *Ostpolitik*, it would very likely have wanted to move forward with an expansion of the Common Market. It, like France, saw British membership in European institutions as a natural boon. While the French wanted

[21] For studies of the origins of the new German foreign policy, see Karl Kaiser, *German Foreign Policy in Transition* (New York: Oxford University Press, 1968); Lawrence Whetten, *Germany's* Ostpolitik (New York: Oxford University Press, 1971).

British membership as a counterweight to Germany, the German government favored British entry as a counterweight to the sorts of policies that France had favored in Europe and that Germany had unwillingly accepted. The Common Agricultural Policy, for example, was highly costly to the German government, which had provided most of the support for its infrastructure. The German government had always seen in Britain a government essentially in favor of creating a free-trade area in Europe—one that would be far more extraversive than the one the French had fostered—and a government also disinclined to accept the sort of *dirigiste* policies pursued by France.

Thus, the coincidence of German and French interests in reviving Europe and expanding the Common Market resulted essentially from policies that were tangentially related to Europeanism, but which also permitted each to achieve a set of complementary goals. Only with regard to their different prognoses for British behavior in Europe did they essentially differ, and here they were both aided by the new British government, elected in mid-1970 under Conservative Edward Heath. Heath sought British membership in Europe for what might well be termed essentially Gaullist motivations.[22] Britain would, through membership in and leadership of the Common Market, be able to pursue a foreign policy with a wider base of support. Moreover, throughout the negotiations concerning British entry, Heath was able to give both the French and the German government the impression that Britain would behave as each expected it would, thus never bringing out the contradictory motivations of the two European governments for British entry.

Two other contextual issues must be specified in outlining the motivations of European political leaders at The Hague in 1969. First, the Soviet invasion of Czechoslovakia in August 1968 had made it clear to European officials that Soviet goals in Europe were essentially unchanged and that the Europeans would have to rely for their security on continued deployment of American troops in Europe and the U.S. commitment in NATO for the foreseeable future.[23] Intra-European squabbles over the nature of American dominance and the desirability of the American linkage therefore no

[22] For details of the negotiations involved in Britain's entry into the European Community, see Uwe Kitzinger, *Diplomacy and Persuasion* (London: Thames and Hudson, 1973).

[23] Michael Tatu argues this in *Le Triangle Washington-Moscou-Pékin et les deux Europes* (Paris: Casterman, 1972).

longer impeded efforts at European unity as they had in the 1960s when de Gaulle had withdrawn French support of the alliance's military command. Second, the Strategic Arms Limitation Talks (SALT) between the United States and Soviet governments had just begun and were raising suspicions within Europe of ultimate super-power objectives. Fearful of eventual superpower condominium over Europe's security options, each of the European governments saw in a revived set of European political institutions the chance to create a European identity that would also make possible an eventual European alternative to the Atlantic connection.[24]

Limitations on Europe's Options

So long as the political compromises among the European govern-ments held up and so long as the contextual issues that formed the background of the meeting at The Hague remained unchanged, vigorous joint action was possible in Europe. Decisions that were taken in Europe after the 1969 summit seemed to point out a growing consensus among responsible European political officials concerning long-term European foreign policy objectives. Europeans seemed to have wanted to take actions that would affirm the growing autonomy of a developing collective European enterprise. What Europeans seemed to have in mind was the old Gaullist vision of a politically unified Europe, free from superpower interference in the internal af-fairs of its societies, and with an attractive core area that could de-velop a special sphere of influence in the Mediterranean area and Africa. Certainly the ad hoc development of the common commercial policy of the European Community pointed in that direction. Special preferential arrangements with developed economies in Europe and with less developed societies in Africa had all been rationalized in terms of Europe's special and historical relationships with associated areas.[25] These commercial arrangements undermined attempts within the GATT to create universal rules for commercial behavior and reflected the European preference for global economic and political balance among large industrial core areas.

If the basic long-term goals of the European government were

24 See Johan J. Holst, "Arms Control and the European Political Process," *Survival* 15, no. 6 (Nov.–Dec. 1973):283–88.

25 See Karl Kaiser, *Europe and the United States: The Future of the Relationship* (Washington, D.C.: Columbia Books, 1973).

clear, fundamental questions remained concerning how these goals would be implemented; and these questions were never squarely confronted. While the Europeans continually affirmed their desire to create an economic and monetary union as a first step to political unification, they never specified what sort of political union they collectively preferred. Thus the entire range of political possibilities, from tight parliamentary democracy to a loose confederacy, remained open. Nor was it clear whether the economic and monetary union would take the form of coordinated national policies or that of integration along functionally specific issue-areas.

Fundamental strategic issues were also ignored. A Europe free from superpower dominance would certainly have to form a security community of its own. Yet military power in Europe remained rudimentary. The French and British nuclear forces existed as a hope around which an eventual European nuclear defense force might be created. For the moment, however, no government was willing to invest in defense expenditures either for high-technology hardware (on a scale that would create a credible deterrent force) or for conventional troops.[26] The issue of who would control an independent nuclear striking force in Europe was never confronted. The lack of military power in Europe was compounded by the lack of symmetry between membership in NATO and the European Community. Not all of the European members of NATO were associated with the Common Market, and one Common Market member (Ireland) did not participate in the military organization. That the major European governments had divergent long-term goals with respect to the security link to the United States was likewise avoided as a contentious issue. But the fact remained that a nonnuclear Germany had to be tied to American security guarantees, regardless of whether the German government was conservative or socialist. It was also clear that a future Labour government in Britain would probably stress the American security connection far more than the current Tory leadership was stressing it.

Finally, the Europeans continuously chose to ignore trends in the international system that crosscut and contradicted their effort to become increasingly autonomous. In particular, they refused to admit that there was a general growth in economic and political interdependence among all of the industrialized economies of the non-

[26] A detailed analysis is provided in John Newhouse, ed., *U.S. Troops in Europe* (Washington, D.C.: The Brookings Institution, 1971).

Communist world, including Japan, Canada, and the United States.[27] This had become most evident in international monetary affairs, where "sensitivity interdependence" had grown remarkably and where none of the industrialized societies was any longer autonomous to pursue domestic, let alone foreign policy, goals.[28] While this general set of developments in international interdependence seemed to many observers to have become inexorable, Europeans (both officially and unofficially) refused even to use the word *interdependence*, arguing that the term was a synonym for continued American economic predominance in Europe.

In spite of these intractable problems, which obstructed any attempt to create an independent European entity, the Europeans took vigorous and concrete action to implement their vision. A monetary union was progressively implemented; most of the members of the European Community chose to restrict the margins within which their parties would be allowed to fluctuate just as the rest of the world seemed to be moving to a regime of flexible rates. The U.S. government certainly helped the Europeans form their monetary coalition by flirting with the presumptive cold war enemies, China and Russia, and by treating the European and Japanese allies as presumptive economic enemies. The successful conclusion of SALT I between the Soviet Union and the United States also facilitated European cooperation by making the Europeans suspicious of superpower goals and fearful that unless they maintained the momentum of intra-European cooperation, they would progressively eliminate any chance to determine their own future.

Momentum in Europe was maintained throughout 1972 and 1973. By the fall of 1972, the expansion of the communities was successfully completed; and, although the referendum in Norway concerning accession had failed, few in Europe doubted that eventually the Norwegians would reverse their position. More important was British ratification of the terms of entry. During the first half of 1973 the Europeans also managed to meet challenges before them exceedingly well. They seemed to be able to respond adequately (by not responding) to Henry Kissinger's "year of Europe" speech by refusing to allow

[27] The best analysis of this remains Richard N. Cooper, *The Economics of Interdependence* (New York: McGraw-Hill, 1968).

[28] See the arguments of Robert O. Keohane and Joseph S. Nye, "World Politics and the International Economic System," in *The Future of the International Economic Order*, ed. C. Fred Bergsten (Lexington, Mass.: Lexington Books, 1973), pp. 115–79.

the U.S. government to manipulate European security and economic relationships. At the opening meeting of the Conference on Security and Cooperation in Europe they managed to present a united front against the Soviet Union and to avoid their worst fear, of succumbing to division brought about by Soviet diplomatic initiatives. While there was some disagreement on Mutual and Balanced Force Reductions and in monetary talks, by and large the Europeans continued to caucus and to maintain unity.

A major fear of the Europeans throughout this period was that of manipulation by the United States. Given the European vulnerability on security issues, they feared that the U.S. government would continue to make monetary and commercial demands that would impede the growth of European economic autonomy and that the United States would threaten to uncouple American defense and European defense if these demands were not met. The European governments realized that as long as they continued both to fear covert threats from the Soviet Union and to be unable to increase their defense expenditures, they were extremely weak on this issue. But they also managed to avoid a linkage between security and economic issues in their diplomatic dealings with the United States and to convince the United States that manipulating such a linkage would be dangerous to all parties.

In summary, the European governments, beginning in 1969 and continuing through 1973, were engaged in a process of negotiation among themselves on expansion of the Common Market as well as on the institutionalization of a set of policies tthat seemed to be creating the basis of a political entity transcending the limited customs union created in the previous decade. At the same time, they successfully confronted both the United States and the Soviet Union in monetary, trade, and security negotiations containing elements that could potentially tear apart their enterprise. A new form of summit diplomacy, not simply among EC governments at The Hague in 1969, in Paris in 1972, and in Copenhagen in 1973, but also—and more frequently—at a bilateral level, seemed to reinforce the tendencies inherent in the collective decisions of 1969.

Europe after the Oil Crisis

The oil crisis seemingly disrupted the high levels of cooperation and recognition of mutual interest that had created a wave of optimism in Europe in the early 1970s. Although the European governments presented an almost solid bloc against the United States on the question of using American supplies and bases in Europe to aid Israel during the 1973 Yom Kippur War, once the Arab governments imposed their oil embargo, the European front fragmented. The disunity in Europe was clear from the beginning of the embargo, as no European government ventured public support of the Netherlands, whose major oil resources had been closed off. As the energy crisis progressed, the European governments apparently were more willing to see the multinational oil companies arrange an equitable distribution of oil resources in Europe than to form a common energy policy of their own, lest they provoke Arab oil-exporting governments. And, since the private distribution of oil created risks with respect to supply, France, Britain, and Germany each began to negotiate separate bargains with various supplier states. These separate deals affected not only the possibility of formulating a common energy policy, but their ramifications severely affected existing common policies as well as the will of the various governments to continue cooperative ventures.

It is clearly the case that at the end of 1973, elements of compromise existed among the EC governments. The different interests of the British, Italian, German, and French governments with regard to a common regional fund and social, environmental, industrial, energy, and agricultural policies provided the basis for a conceivable set of compromises that would benefit each. Moreover, the Community was obviously confronting a dual set of crises: on the one hand, the energy crisis had pervaded national politics in each government; on the other hand, self-imposed deadlines (January 1) existed for agreement on funding a new regional policy. In short, the Community had before it a classical European scenario for making Community-wide policy decisions. Yet none of the traditional Common Market formulas for compromise and decision seemed to work.

Three sets of reasons may be offered to help explain the sudden halt of what has come to be called the "European construction." First, the set of compromises worked out originally in 1969 was undermined by domestic problems in each of the major European governments. Second, there arose a set of international issues that made European cooperation extremely difficult so long as such cooperation implied policies distinct from those being carried out elsewhere in the industrial world, and especially in the United States. Finally, it can be argued that the energy crisis of 1973 did little more than provoke recognition that the vigorous movements of the early years of the 1970s had always disguised an underlying malaise in Europe, which reflected political paralysis in the major European governments as well as political divisions among the core European governments.

It should be recalled that the compromises of 1969 and 1970 that had led to the expansion of the Common Market, the attempt at monetary union, and the effort to coordinate foreign policies, reflected less a consensus on these policies than trade-offs between the member governments, whose principal policy objectives lay elsewhere. By early 1974, the political leadership in Britain, France, and Germany had been in office for from four to five years and had lost the élan that had been present in 1969–70. Heath would soon lose an election and his Tory government would be replaced by a Labour government that had campaigned for renegotiating the terms of British entry into the European Community. In France, Pompidou would soon die and recognition of his declining health had already set off pre-election campaign maneuvering. And Brandt's tenure as chancellor of the Federal Republic of Germany would be limited as well. In summary, domestic political problems in each of the major European governments were no longer conducive to European cooperation. A brief survey of each of these governments should make this clear.

The French government had initially been instrumental in the European *relance* of 1969. For a set of reasons described earlier, Georges Pompidou had been in the vanguard of the European revival. Yet, by 1974 his motivation for pursuing common European goals was no longer evident.[29] While Pompidou had attempted through his European policy to secure domestic political support, he found that his effort had brought no rewards. He and his government had been unable to transfer the popularity in France for Europe to their own policy choices. In a referendum Pompidou had called for in the spring of 1972, approval of British entry into the Economic Community only narrowly passed, since French voters who wished to demonstrate their dislike for Pompidou's regime chose either to abstain from the vote or to vote no. This was made clearer early in 1973 when, in parliamentary elections, the Gaullists lost their overwhelming majority. Unable to free himself from right-wing Gaullists or to secure a new political base, Pompidou and his

[29] See the two supplementary surveys on France that appeared in the *Economist* on Dec. 2, 1972, and Feb. 23, 1974.

government retreated into classical Gaullist rhetoric. A conservative Gaullist prime minister, Pierre Messner, had been appointed to replace the more liberal Chaban-Delmas, and the French government began again to sing the virtues of autonomy, to stress Franco-Soviet ties, and to disclaim the need for European-American cooperation. Having failed in its European venture, and afraid of an eventual electoral loss to a coalition of the Left, the French government hoped that the older Gaullist policy could rally Gaullist supporters and, given its pro-Soviet and anti-American position, split off Communist votes from the Communist-Socialist electoral alliance.

If domestic factors subdued French expectations for Europe, international policy choices served to reinforce the tendency of noncooperation. The pursuit of a common monetary policy, for example, was no longer as urgent as it once had been. The French had fostered such a policy primarily to save the CAP and to present an alternative to European dependence on a dollar standard.[30] By 1974, however, world commodity prices had risen greatly and frequently were higher than target prices. The CAP therefore became less relevant to French internal interests, and the need to maintain relatively fixed exchange rates to support the CAP declined in importance. Since the rest of the world had also been moving toward a regime of flexible exchange rates and since governments everywhere recognized the advantages of this regime in terms of enhanced governmental ability to deal with domestic problems, including inflation, France's withdrawal from participation in the European monetary float had domestic rewards. Moreover, it was not clear whether a common float was still necessary as a means of pressuring the United States on monetary reform, since the presumed advantages to the United States and the dollar in the fixed rate system no longer so obviously obtained. In short, for a series of domestic and international reasons, the French government turned its attention away from its European policy, which no longer seemed to bring domestic political rewards, and toward predominantly internal problems.

A similar situation arose in Germany. Brandt's movement toward Europe in 1969 had originally been motivated by the requirements of a successful *Ostpolitik*. By the end of 1973, however, the Eastern treaties had been successfully negotiated, and it was no longer clear

---

[30] The best general analysis of problems of monetary union in Europe is Lawrance Krause and Walter S. Salant, eds., *European Monetary Unification and Its Implications for the United States* (Washington, D.C.: The Brookings Institution, 1973).

what future existed for the further pursuit of *Ostpolitik*. Not only were there no bases for additional mutual agreements between Germany and the Soviet bloc countries, but *Ostpolitik* began to lose the political glamour that had earlier been attached to it. Domestic critics of Brandt argued that he had given away too much in the treaties that he had negotiated and that, in the meantime, he had neglected domestic policy needs. There was a great deal of truth in that accusation. Even though the Socialist party had gained a majority in parliamentary elections in 1972, it remained in coalition with the Free Democratic party; and the Socialist party was itself split on how far it should move on legislating its program. Left-wing Socialists bucked party discipline and urged the resignation of the chancellor in favor of a more activist leader, and domestic policies against inflation (the dread of German politics) did not seem to deal adequately with what had become a more universal and intractable problem.

The domestic situation in Germany affected the government's European policy in other ways. The government had always been vulnerable on European matters. It was generally regarded as having been the major financial supporter of most European ventures, which had served the interests of other European governments more than those of Germany. The finance minister, Helmut Schmidt, who had ambitions eventually to become chancellor, succumbed to these pressures and argued that the other members of the Economic Community could no longer expect Germany to pay disproportionately for Community projects such as agricultural funds or the regional fund that was being negotiated in the winter of 1973–74. When the French government decided so overtly not to cooperate either in Europe or in a wider arena of advanced industrialized societies on energy policy, the German government's willingness to sacrifice any of its goals to preserve Europe was severely undermined. Not only was the security linkage to the United States a more important continuing element in German foreign policy, but the general global commercial interests of Germany seemed to coincide more with those of Japan and the United States than with those of France. Since the government also believed that it was desirable—if not urgent—to coordinate a policy among oil-consuming countries, its willingness to deal with French intransigence was further reduced.

British domestic problems were evidently even more severe than those of France or Germany. Wage and price controls in Britain in the face of galloping inflation were both ineffective and unpopular, and union pressures on the government's policies were unrelenting. By the winter of 1973, with the coal miners' strike and the oil crisis, it became apparent not only that the Tory government had lost its legitimacy but also that British society, albeit highly divided, was more willing to give in to what were considered legitimate labor demands and to end the domestic paralysis inflicted by the miners' strike than to continue a stringent policy of governmental control.

Although the British economy had apparently not suffered in the first year of British membership in the European Community as Labour critics had predicted it would, the British commitment to EC policies was never very secure. Unwilling to sacrifice balance-of-payments costs that would be involved in adherence to a common monetary policy, the British had elected not to join in the common currency float of the Community. At the same time, sterling suffered a general decline in world financial markets, and this decline only aggravated growing balance-of-payments deficits. By the time the Labour government came to office in early 1974, the British commitment to Common Market policies was highly questionable. Even before the elections had been held, the British government had tried desperately to secure a common regional fund, which would have given Heath the visible reward from membership in the European Community that he had sought. However, the German government had been unwilling to finance the fund on the levels demanded, and the French government had refused to secure a compromise with Germany on funding. Heath chose to veto other Common Market projects until the regional fund was secured, and this action, in late 1973, further brought the Community to stalemate.

A series of domestic and international changes, in short, undermined the set of compromises that had served to relaunch Europe earlier in the 1970s. When European governments chose not to confront the oligopolistic position of Arab oil-exporting countries and when they each feared that skyrocketing oil prices would bring an end to the continuing economic growth they had experienced, the underlying malaise in Europe—which had never disappeared—seemed to overwhelm the European construction. I have elsewhere identified the elements of this malaise, which were not so apparent to observers in early 1973, and it may be useful at this point to recapitulate them.[31]

A major element in the European malaise, especially after the

31 Edward L. Morse, "Why the Malaise," *Foreign Affairs* 51, no. 2 (Jan. 1973): 367–79.

energy crisis, is recognition that in spite of its continuous economic growth and prosperity, Europe remains fundamentally a weak and divided actor in international relations. Self-sufficient in relatively few raw materials and unable to provide autonomously for self-defense, the European governments can no longer be so optimistic about their collective ability to break away from American protection or to compete with the more self-sufficient American economy. This recognition made it extremely difficult to paper over divergent European views not simply on how to deal with the challenge brought on by the Arab countries' announced cut in oil production, but more fundamentally on how to confront the Soviet Union or to cooperate with the United States.

Second, domestic electoral politics continued to intrude into European foreign policy, as noted above. The coordination of policies in Europe has always been a factor affecting the momentum in organizing Europe. When in propitious moments Europeanism has served to reinforce cooperation, Europe has collectively gained. But in 1973–74 domestic and electoral politics in each of the major European states prevented policy cooperation. This disjunction between domestic demands and the requirements of a European political order seems to be increasingly severe. Recent European elections have demonstrated the inexorable involvement of grave economic issues that carry with them significant international elements.

Inflation in all of the European societies is clearly an international issue, but it is one that so affects fundamental domestic policies that the natural option of governments is to deal with it unilaterally. This third element of malaise has been especially the case in Germany, where the specter of inflation has haunted domestic politics since 1923. Pressures for appreciating the exchange rate as one means of controlling inflation have certainly made it difficult to coordinate a common float of European currencies. At the same time, inflationary pressures seem to be built in to modern political systems, given the anticipation of increases in personal income. Since this trend is general, some policy coordination dealing with wage settlements is urgently needed. Paradoxically, however, the need for international cooperation has been crosscut by growing introversion, which makes it difficult to escape the framework of national decision-making.

Other factors contributing to the current malaise in Europe include the difficulties of coordinating policies when nine rather than six sets of vested interests must be taken into account, the continued lack of a European lobby to advance European interests either in the Community or elsewhere, and intra-European political jealousies concerning who is to lead Western Europe. But the most formidable obstacle to European cooperation seems to stem from conditions inherent in modernized societies, the same conditions that have led to a feeling of incapacity within governments to deal effectively with current problems or with an unknown future. Basic to this feeling of incapacity and reinforcing a decreasing ability to govern has been the remarkable and unprecedented web of interdependencies in which governments find themselves.

It is obvious that in almost every policy area, from agriculture to money and energy, activities in one issue-area or actions by any single government affect the domestic and foreign policy options of the others. Interdependence has brought with it not only increasing wealth and other gains for all of Europe but also diminished autonomy for any one political system. The problems of interdependence—choosing either to relinquish sovereign rights by accepting and institutionalizing interdependence, or to lose wealth and welfare benefits by curbing it—are compounded by uncertainties in the governance of modern industrialized societies. Europe's ancient political cultures have provided stability for governments in a period of rapid change and social dislocation. But governments have tended to deal with dislocations through ad hoc daily decision-making, which reinforces attachment to the status quo and prevents governments from thinking about the effects of current policy on future options and from steering a course for the future.

The present crisis in Europe has posed three stark choices before the European governments, each choice carrying benefits as well as costs: (1) independent national action in most fields, (2) joint action within Western Europe, and (3) common and coordinated action among the industrialized societies of the non-Communist world. Pressures exist for each of these options, and the exact compromises among them is by no means clear.

Independent action along national lines now seems to be a likely choice, although in the long run it is also likely to bring with it extremely heavy burdens. The incentives for selecting autonomous action are great. Domestic politics, as we have observed, has now created the strongest tendency for self-reliance since World War II. The crisis in governmental legitimacy, which appears ubiquitous in Europe, motivates each government to take actions that appear to reward it most. This tendency is reinforced by the reliance on bilateral negotiations with oil-supplier governments during the energy crisis, which itself, as argued earlier, forebodes a growing tendency in world politics to emphasize security of sources of supply of raw materials. Independent actions imply the continued fragmentation of Europe. Yet it should be borne in mind that not all of the European governments are likely to opt for a predominantly national course of action. Britain and Italy, the societies with the most severe internal difficulties at the moment, are much more likely to lead the movement toward fragmentation than are Germany, with its economic and military ties to the United States; France, with its commitment to tie Germany's hands in spite of its own domestic difficulties; or the Benelux countries and Denmark, with their natural economic ties to Germany. Fragmentation caused by nationally autonomous actions is thus likely to be limited by crosscutting tendencies, which will preserve a basis for future common action when and if domestic conditions change in Europe.

Joint action limited to the Western European governments would clearly be preferable to fragmentation, even if it offers a second-best solution.[32] But a new relaunching of Europe, while not out of the question, seems highly unlikely. One ought, however, to be cautious in predicting its future probability. Changes in mood in Europe have been abrupt in recent years. The pessimism in Europe of the late 1960s changed rather radically to optimism by 1970, just as the recent optimism was quickly dispelled. After the oil crisis, national leadership in Britain, France, and Germany was weak. New elections in each of these societies might well bring to the fore an unexpected vitality, even if the opportunity for compromise among a set of differential but symbiotically related policies does not now appear to exist. However, it also appears that even such a compromise would have only limited viability. Interdependence between Europe and other industrialized societies, especially the United States, may well be so great that the pressure for a wider base for common or coordinated action may prevail.

The third option, joint decision-making and consultations among all of the advanced industrialized societies of the non-Communist world, appears to me to be the most rational and best choice.[33] To

[32] Many observers would find this a best rather than a second-best solution. See, for example, David Calleo, "The Political Economy of Allied Relations: The Limits of Interdependence," in *Retreat from Empire?* ed. Robert E. Osgood (Baltimore: Johns Hopkins University Press, 1973), pp. 207–40.

[33] For a good argument concerning joint management, see Miriam Camps,

be sure, the fear of American domination in any generalized arrangement will exist, especially in the French government. But there are good reasons to select this option. Most obvious is that the major domestic and international problems confronted by the industrialized societies are, in two senses, common. First, they are shared insofar as these societies are linked to one another in interdependent relations and there is little likelihood that any subgroup of these societies can handle them adequately without harmonizing policies within the wider arena. This holds for monetary, trade, energy, and environmental problems. Second, they are shared in the sense that the industrialized societies have developed similar economic, political, and social structures, so that the handling of problems within any one society will have implications for their handling elsewhere.

Another argument that could be marshaled for a more general framework for cooperation relates, paradoxically, to possibilities within Europe itself. It can be argued that European unity may well be best fostered within a more general framework that includes North America and Japan as well. Such a framework would avoid splits within Europe concerning the desirability of the American connection. Germany in particular would not be pulled alternatively in Atlanticist and European directions. Moreover, even within such a general framework, the Europeans could be encouraged to caucus together so as to prevent manipulation by the United States. Indeed, they might better be able to formulate a European identity in this wider framework than they would should they consciously attempt to pursue a policy distinct from or opposite to that of the United States.

While joint action among the industrialized societies is likely to prove the most efficient and rational way to proceed, obstacles to it may well be too great.[34] Not only would Europeanists have to relinquish claims to continue to provide the elements of a separate European identity, but, equally important, the U.S. government would have to act with good faith and accept European intransigence, which would likely crop up from time to time. Given recent American impatience with European decision-making processes, it is not clear how easy it would be for the United States to act in

---

The Management of Interdependence: A Preliminary View, Council Papers on International Affairs, no. 4 (New York: Council on Foreign Relations, 1974).

34 Stanley Hoffmann has argued that this "trilateral" approach is both inefficient and impractical in "Choices," *Foreign Policy*, no. 15 (Fall 1973), pp. 3–42.

such a way as to keep a side-based set of consultative mechanisms operable, but it certainly ought to be worth a try.

Predictions concerning which of these options is most likely to be followed is difficult. The stakes for all governments involved, be they European or extra-European, remain extremely high. Only if the current crisis deepens will it become likely that habits and relationships built up over the past quarter-century will be relinquished, since they have also brought with them unprecedented economic prosperity and military security. The elements of compromise either within Europe or between Europe and the United States still exist. The political will for further cooperative ventures, which is now lacking, might well reappear as a new set of political leaders comes to power in Europe as well as the United States.

The Impact of International Economic Factors on the Conduct of Foreign Policy

Fritz Bock

T HOSE who are familiar with the situation of world politics will consider the relations between the United States and the Soviet Union—which, ever since the two "summit meetings," have become more definite, and which from the beginning, have been predominantly economic in nature—as constituting a warning that Western Europe might become isolated before it can exercise an influence on world politics corresponding to its economic strength. "Western Europe still represents only an enormous concentration of economic power, but not a political factor, which, as a subject of equal standing, might outbalance the American protective power or the neighboring Russian superpower."[1]

Yet if one sets out from the certainly bold hypothesis—as was done by a European Community (EC) spokesman—that "a rational foreign policy no longer depends on the number of soldiers or the state of armament of a nation, but is based rather on the economic capacity and, consequently, on the trade volume of a country, the European Community, being the most important trading partner in the world, certainly exercises an eminently political function."[2] Apart from the common development policy pursued from the very beginning, the common trade policy, effective since January 1, 1970, constitutes the concrete start of a common foreign policy. It is assumed, for example, that the European Community will coordinate the attitudes of the member countries within the General Agreement on Tariffs and Trade (GATT) and the International Monetary Fund (IMF)

[1] Dalma, "Bis auf Weiteres auf dem Abstellgleis," *Die Presse* (Vienna), June 30–July 1, 1973. All translations into English have been made by the author.
[2] P. Bahr, "Handel und Händel zwischen Ost und West," *Europa-Archiv*, May 1973, p. 173.

and, to a certain extent, within the Organization for European Cooperation and Development (OECD), the Economic Commission for Europe (ECE), the United Nations Conference on Trade and Development (UNCTAD), and the International Economic Association (IAE), and will adopt a concerted stance[3]—an assumption that undoubtedly is, for the time being, highly optimistic.

Likewise, Secretary General Brezhnev, in his address to the Congress of Soviet Trade Unions on March 3, 1972, referred to the "real situation" in Europe, which had to be recognized, and also mentioned in this context the European Community. His formulations have been used repeatedly by other Soviets, and at the end of August 1973, the secretary general of the Council for Mutual Economic Assistance (Comecon), Nicolai Faddeyev, contacted an acting chairman of the Council of Ministers of the European Community. Although it appears to be too early to infer therefrom a radical realignment of policy on the part of the Soviet Union and the Eastern bloc toward the European Community (at present a recognition of the European Community as a subject of international law by the Eastern countries appears as unlikely as contracts "between the blocs"), it becomes apparent that the attitude toward the Common Market, which set in some time ago, is continuing. The improvement in long-term economic cooperation between the West and East European countries should also be an important issue of the Conference on Security and on Cooperation in Europe (CSCE). Thus, the *Ostpolitik*, which is now primarily pursued by the Federal Republic of Germany, will be increasingly multilateralized owing to the harmonization and joint proceeding of the nine member countries of the European Community. The scope of such a process will, however, depend on the success of West Germany's *Ostpolitik*. In this context it should be borne in mind that Bonn's *Ostpolitik* is a highly controversial issue within the conservative circles of Western Europe in particular. The former German chancellor, Brandt, who in the end failed owing to his *Ostpolitik*, is blamed for having sold everything while receiving almost nothing in return. Not only could a closer cooperation of the European Community and Comecon, which would have to be based on the principle of reciprocity, contribute to European security; but by taking into account imperative economic

[3] See R. Dahrendorf, "Europäische Alternativen," *Wiener Schriften*, no. 36 (Apr. 1972), p. 11.

necessities it could bring the economic blocs, which today are still isolated, closer together as part of an intensified integration of world economies.

President Nixon's address of May 3, 1973, on current world affairs also reflects this crystallization of international economic politics as a supporting element—as an instrument for peace—in the concept of foreign policy.[4] The Europeans, however, are faced with the fundamental question: Can the principle of the Atlantic unity of defense and security be made compatible with the economic policy of the European Community, which is becoming increasingly regional in nature? The American euphoria of the late 1950s and early 1960s, which was focused on the hope of a quick formation of a solid West European bloc, gave way to the fear of the consequences of the development of a European economic area, which the Americans in some respects consider "discriminatory, introverted, unfair in the fields of trade and monetary policies, and unable or unwilling to share on an equal basis with the Atlantic partner the burden of defending the free world."[5] This reveals the great extent to which relations between Europe and the United States are at present determined by economic factors, such as the international monetary situation and the differences between the two large economic blocs regarding their trade policies. However, the relationship between Europe and the United States is not governed exclusively by economic issues. In order to safeguard its security, Europe is in need of the military protection and the undiminished engagement of the United States. There is certainly some justification for the presumption that the Soviet-American détente might lead to a deterioration of the traditional West European security system. The Strategic Arms Limitation Talks (SALT) agreements might weaken the nuclear guarantee, and sooner or later a détente would have to result in a reduction of American troops in Europe; the Mutual Forces Reduction (MFR) negotiations only support this tendency.

The further development of the relationship between the United States and the Soviet Union, which was again emphasized by the summit conferences in 1973 and 1974, has escalated the European concern that the course has been set and that the United States will increasingly shift to bilateral arrangements which frequently will be strongly influenced by domestic tendencies in Washington and

[4] See "Die Internationalisierung der amerikanischen Wirtschaftspolitik," *Neue Züricher Zeitung*, May 6, 1973.

[5] "Der Eigenwert der Handelspolitik," *Neue Züricher Zeitung*, Apr. 1, 1973.

Moscow and which will tend to anticipate discussions on the multilateral scene at a later date. Whether or not this European concern is justified, whether it will grow or diminish, might essentially depend on the long-called-for reorganization of the Atlantic alliance and its adjustment to the "new realities."[6] The increasing impact of economic factors on foreign policies can, in any case, no longer be ignored.

Political Expectations in West and East as a Consequence of Intensified Interbloc Trade and Cooperation

The Relationship between the United States and the Soviet Union

President Nixon's visit to Moscow in May 1972 paved the way for contacts between the United States and the Soviet Union. What has followed has confirmed the fact that countries whose economic and political conditions are diametrically opposed can bring about economic and cultural agreements more quickly and easily than disarmament treaties. The latter, so far, have been concluded within a limited scope and have reduced the arms race only to a small extent, if at all.

One has to be aware of this fact since, after all, it results from the nature of human relations and can be traced back to the beginnings of the history of mankind. Power politics is a reality and cannot be assessed by moral standards. It would be a fatal mistake to believe that the striving for power might one day disappear from human life. Nobody should ever struggle for such a utopia, since power as such is the instrument of order. The policy of the Soviet Union is based on its strength, and one must never expect that Moscow—under any circumstances whatever—would be willing to cede

[6] On April 23, 1973, in his analysis of European-American relations, Henry Kissinger proceeded from the fact that the political, military, and economic issues in transatlantic relations were "tied together by reality" and that the global interests and responsibilities of the United States and the regional interests of the European allies need not necessarily be identical. Yet, despite the criticisms made with regard to several aspects of the European integration policy (see, for example, the address made by Secretary of Commerce Peter G. Peterson, Jan. 18, 1973), Kissinger emphasized that the United States planned to continue to support European integration as a component of the Atlantic partnership and would not withdraw its armed forces from Europe unilaterally. However, the United States expected that it would be met on a basis of reciprocity and that each ally would accept a fair share in the common defense burden.

even the smallest portion of its acquired power. But it would be equally wrong to conclude from this fact that Moscow might intend to start another world war. The striving for peace is not incompatible with the desire to strengthen one's own power. The development of nuclear weapons—an expansion and increase of military potential that fifty years ago would have been inconceivable—eventually led to the "balance of terror" predicted by Winston Churchill, which in all probability will render another world war impossible. This balance is not in contradiction to the fact of locally limited wars (in the Middle and Far East); they are basically an outlet for maintaining the existing balance of power. Hence disarmament conferences will be successful only if they do not effect any change in this balance. For Europe this means, in concrete terms, unrestricted maintenance of the military presence of the United States in Western Europe and absolute American nuclear protection in this area. It cannot be denied that the European contribution to its own defense capacity ought to be larger than it actually is.

Let us now consider the economic aspect. On July 8, 1972, the conclusion of an arrangement between the United States and the Soviet Union was announced, according to which the Soviet Union, in the course of the following three years, would purchase cereals and forage valued at $750 million. Only a few weeks later this amount was raised to $1,000 million. This is the most comprehensive trade agreement in the field of agriculture ever made between two countries. The fact that Russia, after over fifty years of Communist rule, is time and again forced to import cereals proves the failure of the collectivization of agriculture. The United States is primarily interested in importing those raw materials which it lacks or whose natural supply it does not wish to exhaust. Above all, this holds true for natural gas, enormous quantities of which have been discovered in Siberia. At present, the Russian need of supplies from the United States by far exceeds the American demand for supplies from the Soviet Union. It is estimated that in the next years the favorable United States balance of trade with the Soviet Union will show the advantageous ratio of 3 to 1, which might change in favor of the Soviet Union once the deliveries of natural gas have begun. This is a new development which will affect the monetary sector. The Eastern countries have no substantial convertible currencies at their disposal. Their hard currency assets stem almost exclusively from the proceeds of their export industries. This means that the major part of West-East trade continues to be barter trade. The industrial exports of the Eastern countries are limited in scope because of the inferior quality of the Eastern industrial products and the absence of technical service facilities. If the Soviet Union plans to intensify the exploitation and export of its natural resources—in particular, of natural gas and crude oil—it will substantially improve its liquidity. This will greatly stimulate the export of industrial goods and of know-how from West to East. Furthermore, Russia's enormous potential in this field could for some time satisfy the increasing West European energy demands.

The 1972 agreement on the settlement of World War II liabilities and postwar indebtedness constituted an additional basis for new trade agreements. Moreover, Soviet experts are of the opinion that transactions in the range of thousands of millions of dollars could be carried out if the mutual preferences became fully effective.[7] This might overstate Russia's export possibilities, since recent experience with tariff and nontariff trade barriers shows that the Soviet Union has lost much of its importance in the field of trade.[8] Apart from food and forage supplies, the Soviet Union is interested in American technological achievements, particularly in computers and agricultural machinery. "An accumulation of agreements of all kinds and of varying significance, surging like a torrent,"[9] could be observed within a period of less than two years. They range from consular issues to arrangements governing cooperation in the fields of public health, medical research, environmental protection, science and technology, from the joint exploration and exploitation of space for peaceful purposes, including a joint space flight planned for 1975, to the agreements on the prevention of accidents on the high seas. In addition, at the second summit meeting an agreement was concluded on cooperation in the usage of atomic energy for peaceful purposes, particularly of controlled nuclear fusion. This is a field in which the West European countries find it difficult to unite because

[7] An influential group in the U.S. Senate makes the concession of this trade clause dependent on initial steps by the Soviet Union regarding its emigration policy; the trade-unions object to such concessions toward the Soviet Union for basic political reasons and out of fear that they might have a negative sociopolitical effect on the American worker.

[8] See "Vor einem Handelsboom?" *Finanz und Wirtschaft*, Apr. 4, 1973. In 1972, the American administration granted export licenses to the Soviet Union in the amount of $1,700 million, and over 2,500 American entrepreneurs have submitted individual suggestions for business transactions to Moscow.

[9] C. Gasteyger, "Weltmächte und Weltordnung," *Europa-Archiv*, Aug. 25, 1973, p. 541.

they are faced with both overt and hidden resistance on the part of their American ally. There is some speculation that the Soviet attitude is, among other things, determined by the view that what they call the influential circles in the United States had realized the increasing importance of their energy problems and had unemotionally assessed the advantages of cooperation with the Soviet Union. The changes in the American policy toward the Soviet Union since the beginning of the 1970s are considered to be a logical consequence of a realistic appraisal by the American administration of U.S. strength against the background of the energy problem.

Secretary of State Henry Kissinger has defined the U.S. policy as aiming at the incorporation of the agreements reached with the Soviet Union since May 1972 into a gradually tightening web of manifold commitments in order to influence the Soviet attitude in foreign affairs in terms of greater self-restraint, joint responsibility, and cooperation. In addition to the immediate economic advantages of West-East cooperation, the West is regarded as having substantive political advantages in that an intensified cooperation will lead to a certain degree of interdependence and, eventually, to a higher degree of integration.[10] C. A. Andreae sees some relationship between economic cooperation and détente.

Cooperation requires an adjustment of the systems of commercial laws, especially of the laws governing patent and license trade in East and West. The granting of licenses to the East will be useful and successful only if they are protected by contract against abuse and if, at the same time, a license is financially advantageous and necessary for both parties. This, however, makes it necessary for the licensee to establish a better competitive position vis-à-vis other Eastern enterprises of the same category. Market competition has not yet become identical with a capitalistic economic pattern. However, the introduction of the concept of competition in the Eastern economic process constitutes a step toward greater liberties for the customer and citizen. It is a step toward East-West rapprochement.[11]

---

[10] See ibid., p. 546: The basic difference between the American and the Soviet views on the conduct of foreign policy has been described by Nixon along the following lines: The Americans consider international tensions abnormal and, therefore, attempt to settle them as quickly as possible. In contrast, the Soviet Union regards such tensions as a projection of the conflict of rivaling social systems to the interstate level. Thus, in the Soviet view tensions are something natural and unavoidable; to take advantage of them and possibly benefit from them is considered a perfectly normal policy.

[11] "Ost-West-Kooperation—ein Weg zur Befriedigung Europas," *Wirtschaftsdienst*, Aug. 1969, p. 443.

Andreae cites other examples of supposedly far-reaching effects of the license trade on the Eastern economic system and on Eastern ideology in order to prove that the economic West-East cooperation resulting from common economic interests might perhaps lead to the political development aimed at by the West.[12] Thus, intensification of economic relations with the Soviet Union ought to be regarded as a political instrument that no doubt is also based on a concept aiming at long-term effects and goals since it would be unreasonable and politically irresponsible to demand cooperation solely for the sake of short-term economic profits.

So much about the advocates of the so-called theory of convergence. At this point a forthright statement must be made regarding this theory. The division of our world into the two spheres of Western democracy and the Communist social order, or of the social market organization and planned economy, which dominate the political world scene is, like all things in human life, subject to natural and permanent changes. In Stalin's times the cold war prevailed. Nikita Khrushchev gave way to the principle of coexistence, that is, to the mutual recognition of the two social systems based on the status quo, above all in Europe. From this developed, last but not least, stimulated by the technological development, the need for close economic contacts, which finally resulted in an intensified economic intercourse. This led in the Eastern countries to a growing economic intrabloc cooperation and to a substantially greater Eastern bloc emphasis on the countries' economic interests, above all on trade interests.

The great number of trade agreements between West and East and the resulting increasing trade volume, whose limits have already been pointed out, were the natural consequences of this evolution. Furthermore, there arose the necessity for certain adjustments within the system of planned economy, adjustments designed to improve the competitiveness of the Communist national economies in the world market by means of increased productivity and of a more liberal handling of certain aspects of business administration.

This development resulted in the so-called theory of convergence. What is the essence of this theory? It says that because of the mutual recognition of the sociopolitical systems and the need for intensified economic intercourse, the two economic systems, namely, social mar-

[12] Ibid., p. 447. See also H. D. Schoen, "Systemkonvergenz durch Lizenzkooperation zwischen Ost- und Westeuropa," *Wirtschaftspolitische Blätter*, Mar. 1970, p. 171.

ket and planned, will increasingly converge. Eventually they will
show little divergence and, finally, will end up in a mixed composite
of the two systems. To give an example, the proponents of the convergence theory claim that because of technological progress and the
need of both blocs for an intensified economic intercourse, the bases
of and the necessities for an international trade policy and a modern
industrial management are resembling each other to an ever increasing degree. This concept misses a crucial point. The social
market economy is based on the principle of private property, on
the entrepreneur's own responsibility, and on the free and independent policy of the trade-unions. The system of planned economy
rejects the idea of private ownership of the means of production,
as well as in trade and agriculture, and permits private initiative
only to a very limited extent. The principle of a state-controlled
economy is also maintained in countries like Yugoslavia. However,
according to the principle that the employees are the owners of and
responsible for their enterprises, a system has been introduced which
in its appearance and in nothing but its appearance somewhat re-
sembles the cooperative principle. The production programs of
such enterprises are also subject to approval of the authorities.

If we apply the convergence theory to the West, it becomes evident
that here too it fails the test of the realities. If, for instance, government licenses are required in a Western foreign trade system, this is
done only for reasons of bilaterality vis-à-vis the Eastern trading
partner and not as a matter of principle. Nor does the system of
nationalized industries, which plays an important part, particularly
in Austria, conflict with the principles of a social market economy;
these enterprises are organized under the Austrian corporation law,
according to which the rights of the state, as the owner, do not go
beyond those of any private shareholder. However, problems of
industrial management are subject to the private sphere, whereas in
the system of planned economy such problems in particular are
under strict central control by the authorities.

Thus it becomes evident that the so-called theory of convergence is
not valid. This opinion coincides in all points with political convic-
tions in the East, where it has been pointed out repeatedly and em-
phatically that there is not the slightest intention of watering down
the present system. The Eastern economists and politicians continually stress the point that all development trends within the system of
planned economy have to be incorporated into and subjected to the
principles governing this system. This clearly stated position is

not surprising for, in reality, there exists no such thing as a liberalization of communism, since any liberalization would inevitably mean the end of communist society. The same holds true for the West. A social market economy is possible only in countries embracing the democratic form of government as we know it, that is, in a system in which political forces can develop freely within a multiple party system. The system of planned economy, however, calls for a one-party system as its integral political basis. On neither side of the demarcation line between the two political and social orders is there the slightest intention of deviating from these principles.

The question of convergence versus coexistence thus answers itself. The simultaneous existence of the two political and economic systems, their mutual acceptance, and the principle of noninterference are the characteristics of coexistence. Coexistence is also the prerequisite for a reasonably peaceful development in the world.

At this point I would like to comment briefly on my native country, Austria. Austria is a neutral state. The freedom of the political profession of democracy in the Western sense, and the social market economy, is in no way restricted by the status of Austria's neutrality under international law. The Austrian neutrality is a condition of the State Treaty of 1955, and not an element of it. The neutral status obliges Austria to refrain from interfering with the concerns of other parties and, at the same time, protects Austria from outside interference. Thus it is a manifestation of coexistence in terms of international law. Since Austria is a purely Western country on account of its domestic structure, its existence also disproves the claim of convergence.

These reflections coincide fully with the Soviet Union's expectations. The Soviet Union considers its agreements with the West "first and foremost to mean recognition as an equal partner of the United States, something it had always aimed at."[13] In other words, its goal is primarily political.

The arms race has driven both superpowers, at enormous costs and risks, to accumulate a military potential hitherto unknown. This has not resulted in a higher degree of independence or flexibility for them. On the contrary, now that they have reached the climax of their power, their security is based on cooperation and not on rivalry. The efforts of the Soviet Union to reach a political arrangement with the West on the state level went hand in hand

[13] Gastgeyer, p. 546.

with the ideological backup of its "policy of détente" by propagating an intensified class struggle.[14] It cannot yet be determined to what extent this has nourished the distrust of many potential cooperating partners in the West or to what degree it has counteracted the Soviet economic interests. Also, the consequences of the Soviet-American summit arrangements for all minor partners in the West and the East cannot yet be appraised. Do they mean a new basis implying changes or even losses? Does rapprochement in the field of foreign trade improve the integration effect in the East and the West, or do pinpointed bilateralities among individual Eastern and Western partners rather result in a stagnation, a weakening of solidarity, of voluntary interdependence among the members of the European Community and Comecon?[15]

The question has been frequently raised in recent years in connection with European integration whether the European Community, as it was initially established by the 1956 Treaty of Rome, and as it has developed under the 1960 European Free Trade Association (EFTA) Treaty and the so-called 1972 Global Treaty, will have a real chance in the future or whether it will break up again due to internal differences or external interference. My answer to this question can be anticipated: the structure of European integration is stable and will continue to develop and to consolidate. This statement requires proof. First of all, it must be pointed out that once created, a large economic area, within which trade can develop free from tariff barriers and protectionist institutions, can never be split up again into individual parts without severe damage to their economy. In other words, the internal exchange of goods and services, both within the European Community and the remaining EFTA members, as well as between these two integration areas, has reached such dimensions that nobody can reasonably contemplate the reintroduction of trade barriers. European integration is, however, not

[14] Time and again one can read statements like the following one, made by Brezhnev: "While we are pressing for the enforcement of the principle of peaceful coexistence, we are, at the same time, aware of the fact that successes in this important sphere do in no way mean to us a weakening of our ideological struggle. On the contrary, we ought to be prepared for an intensification of that struggle, as well as for the fact that it is transformed to an ever increasing degree into a bitter fight between the two social systems" (*Pravda*, June 27, 1972, quoted in F. St. Larrabee, "Die sowjetische Politik in Osteuropa und das Problem der Entspannung," *Europa-Archiv*, Apr. 25, 1973, p. 280).

[15] O. R. Liess, "Supermächte und West-Osthandel," *Die Industrie*, June 29, 1973, p. 20.

confined to trade. There also exists within the European Community a common market organization in the field of agriculture. Complicated and in need of reform as this organization may be, it would be impossible for the European Community to abstain from a joint control of agriculture, since this would lead to grave disturbances. Common external economic borders urgently require a great number of additional regulations going beyond trade and agriculture. The Treaty of Rome and numerous additional agreements within the European Community already contain pertinent provisions. The monetary community is in a state of great difficulty and in urgent need of development. But also within the free trade area, common regulations are bound to develop, above all to avoid competitive distortions. This means that the West European integration has become a permanent institution with which the world must reckon and which the Soviet Union takes into account in pursuance of a highly realistic policy (see the above-quoted Brezhnev speech of February 1972).

The Relationship between the European Community and Comecon

In the European Community the member countries execute their sovereignty jointly in those spheres in which they waive their sectional rights. Comecon has the character of an international organization without any commitments toward the so-called interested members. In contrast to the European Community, which as a customs union has from the outset aimed at establishing common foreign relations, the status of Comecon—its goal being to coordinate production—has no external relevance. Although the range of equal or similar competences is extremely limited at present, the European Community has declared that it is willing, in principle, to cooperate with Comecon. "We aspire to a tight interlacing of Eastern and Western Europe," Dahrendorf says, and he continues: "The stronger we are interconnected, the greater the interest will be in peaceful relations."[16] Thus a great number of common economic interests oblige the parties concerned to maintain cooperation and to avoid possible problems and tensions. "Even the best security system is sterile, unless the interested parties are connected by numerous long-term, common, interdependent economic interests."[17] It has

[16] Dahrendorf, p. 18.

[17] J. Bognár, "EWG, EFTA, COMECON—Bilanz und Chancen," *Wiener Schriften*, no. 36 (Apr. 1972), p. 29.

been observed that small Comecon members have often taken the initiative in their relations with the Western free-enterprise countries. These initiatives have now been taken over by the Soviet Union as the supreme body of Comecon. Hungary, Rumania, and later on particularly Poland and the German Democratic Republic have experimented with new forms of cooperation with Western democratic partners. That the concepts of industrial coproduction, third-country transactions, and joint ventures are no longer unknown in East-West trade may be attributed to these countries.[18] Although Eastern bloc reorganizations ("complex program") have been underway since 1971 with the goal of intensified integration, it must be borne in mind that at the 26th Comecon meeting in July 1972, Kosygin emphasized the Soviet position that "to us integration is not only an economic question but also an important factor in the development of the socialist system."[19] This is again a rebuff of the Western proponents of the convergence theory. Thus it becomes apparent that the Soviet policy of détente aims at keeping the Eastern bloc in a rigid interdependence under Soviet hegemony, in order to enable it to benefit from all advantages of an increased technological and economic cooperation resulting from the improved climate of West-East relations.

Since January 1, 1973, bilateral cooperation in the field of bartering, in particular the conclusion of trade agreements between the European Community and the socialist countries, has not been possible. Pursuant to Article 113 of the European Economic Community Commission (EEC) Treaty, the common trade policy is directed in accordance with uniform principles. So far, however, in relations with countries with planned economies, the "classical" instruments of foreign trade policy contained in that article (alteration of tariff rates, conclusion of tariff and trade agreements, unification of the liberalization measures, export policy, measures for the protection of trade) are not accorded the same importance as cooperation agreements. Thus a number of EC countries recently concluded such cooperation agreements; these carefully took into consideration the obligatory range of a common trade policy and, for this reason, were not even the subject of consultation procedure within the European Community. The Soviet Union is thus doubtlessly given ample opportunity to play off the EC partners one against the other.

---

[18] See O. R. Liess, "Von der Konfrontation zur Kooperation," *Die Industrie*, Sept. 28, 1973, p. 27.

[19] Quoted in St. Larrabee, p. 277.

In making efforts to reach separate solutions through bilateral cooperation agreements and their institutionalized, so-called mixed commissions, the Soviet Union envisages two objectives: on the one hand, it appears as though the Soviet Union intended to check the "treaty-making power" of the EEC by endeavoring to incorporate as much as possible into these corporation agreements, which do not fall within the competence of the European Community; on the other hand, the more the Western countries yield to the Eastern demands for most-favored-nation treatment and for liberalization, the more trade with Eastern Europe will be conducted outside of tariffs and quotas. In response, the EEC Commission has drawn up a proposal for the Council of Ministers calling for a community information and consultation procedure for EC agreements with the Eastern bloc countries, which would facilitate a coordination of the cooperation policy. It is of the utmost importance to ensure that the economic relations with the East do not bypass the European Community. The fact that Comecon Secretary General Faddeyev established contacts in the fall of 1973 reveals that such a practice under the banner of détente might be incorporated into Soviet policy. However, for the time being, direct negotiations, not to mention the conclusion of contracts, between Comecon and the European Community are hardly to be expected, since Comecon lacks, to a great extent, the necessary institutions and competences.

The projections of the United Nations Economic Commission for Europe proceed from the assumption that the commercial intercourse for the whole of Europe will increase at a relatively rapid pace.[20] Whereas it is expected that West European exports to the East computed on the basis of 1965–67 will have increased fivefold by 1980, Comecon is expected to expand the volume of its exports to the West fourfold. Due to the low starting position—in Europe East-West trade constitutes less than 4 percent of world trade—the total volume increases slowly.[21] However, it is estimated that during the period from 1970 to 1985 the number of cooperation contracts between the two systems will rise more than tenfold and that the economic East-

20 See M. Schmitt, "Die wirtschaftliche Zusammenarbeit zwischen EWG und RGW," *Wirtschaftsdienst*, Dec. 1972, p. 660.

21 The small volume can be partly explained by two factors: First, interbloc economic relations were for many decades impeded by an embargo of the NATO countries under the strict control of the United States; now that the United States has joined in the competition for East European markets, these relations have become largely liberalized. Second, the competitiveness of East European production is limited in Western markets.

West exchange will amount to between 33 and 50 percent of this figure. There is a growing desire to secure resulting economic advantages by means of military and political guarantees covering all of Europe to the extent to which the economic exchange—trade, cooperation, and coproduction—between East and West increases. Exporters, above all if they act as creditors, require a certain degree of security in order to become actively engaged in business transactions. Therefore, European export intensive countries are particularly interested in pertinent interbloc military, economic, and political agreements concluded between the various governments. "Economy has indeed often paved the way for politics," says Prof. M. Schmitt, and he continues: "Even at a time when neither a friendly attitude toward the East nor a new *Ostpolitik* existed, the economic interests established the contacts with the trading partners in the East under the most trying circumstances and maintained them despite many political strains. We have thus contributed within our range of possibilities, be it only to a modest degree, to paving the way for urgent developments from which politics could benefit later on."[22] One could add that this constitutes another example of the fact that economists are far from being at their wits' ends, even though politicians have given up all hope.

The Economic Components of the Revival
of the Atlantic Partnership

The "year of Europe," 1973, proclaimed by President Nixon after his reelection in November 1972, and Henry Kissinger's appeal for the revival of the Atlantic partnership in April 1973 constituted a call to the allies to engage in a constructive dialogue which, according to the American idea, should deal with the monetary, trade, and security problems of the alliance under the guiding principle of joint responsibility and a just distribution of the burden. The development of a broad political perspective would permit the reconciliation of differences in the interest of achieving higher objectives. This concept manifests the American "package thinking"— that is, the interlocking of political and economic concerns. Thus President Nixon, in his 1973 message on the State of the World, expressed the idea of matching, by means of multilateral solutions,

22 "Ökonomische Perspektiven in der Ostpolitik," *Aussenpolitik*, Apr. 1971, p. 193.

the effects of the American military presence in Europe against the American balance of payments in such a way that it would make practically no difference whether the troops were stationed in Europe or in America.

Consequently, the European Community finds itself in the complex situation of having to operate, so to speak, simultaneously on the "inner and outer fronts." It constitutes a challenge to Western Europe to continue the development of the European Community from the viewpoint of integrating its members and, at the same time, to give them a distinct profile to the outside.[23] However, the various stages of the European-American dialogue also stimulate intensified West European efforts to harmonize and to develop a profile of the community of the Nine vis-à-vis the United States. It will be important for the harmonization of the attitude of the European Community toward the United States that the member countries define their place in world affairs, particularly with regard to the Soviet-American relationship. "There can be no question of creating a third independent power center between the United States and the Soviet Union at equidistance from the two others, and of equal standing. Within an interdependent alliance system with common goals, West Europe and the United States have the same basic concept of human rights and of democratic liberties. Therefore, the policy of the Western Europe of the Nine will show qualitatively different features."[24] The monetary and trade systems within which international relations have developed after World War II were determined to a high degree by the United States as the leading economic power. The United States is still the supreme economic power, but, at least in the field of foreign economy, its leading role is no longer uncontested. Consequently, monetary and trade problems play a decisive part in the transatlantic dialogue.

Monetary Problems

The acute crises of the international monetary system in 1971 and 1973 climaxed a long-term development during the course of which the structural inadequacy of the postwar monetary system became apparent. The agreement reached at Bretton Woods, based on the

[23] See E. Thiel, "Dollarkrise und Bündnispolitik," *Europa-Archiv*, June 10, 1973, p. 373.

[24] Günther van Well, "Die Europäische politische Zusammenarbeit in der aussenpolitischen Sicht der Bundesrepublik Deutschland," *Europa-Archiv*, Sept. 10, 1973, p. 583.

strong U.S. position in international trade and monetary relations after World War II, led to a monetary system within which the U.S. dollar served as the principle currency of intervention in order to guarantee a structure of stable exchange rates.

This preeminent position of the dollar enabled the United States—unlike other countries—to compensate for its balance-of-payments deficits in its own currency, that is, with the printing press. During the period of scarce dollar reserves because of the enormous demand for capital on the part of Europe and the developing countries and to the limited convertibility of currencies—this system worked well. The massive conversion of French dollar balances into gold in the late 1960s and finally the deterioration of the international competitive situation of the United States necessitated an ever increasing number of bilateral standstill agreements, swap arrangements, the granting of standby credits, etc., in order to protect the dollar. These measures led to a substantial loss of confidence in the American currency, which was gradually overcome when the U.S. balance of trade became favorable toward the end of 1973. In this context it must be borne in mind that it was precisely American support through the Marshall Plan which turned the war-stricken countries into keen competitors, and that America, due to its commitments in world politics and development aid, had to bear extraordinary burdens by itself. The world should never forget that. Nevertheless, the Bretton Woods system clearly reflects hegemonial traits. Within the International Monetary Fund, which through recommendation should ensure equilibrium in national balances of payments, the United States enjoys a prominent position in the decision-making bodies. The dollar, based on the American economic potential, came to assume a key position as a leading and reserve currency in international trade and monetary transactions. Once Western Europe and Japan had acquired economic strength, the United States could no longer pursue the policy of "benign neglect" of its balance of payments.[25] The difficulties in connection with the reorganization of the monetary system are not only due to the necessity of finding or further developing new instruments to replace the dollar in its function as a reserve currency on a long-term basis. New mechanisms of adjustment in the international monetary system and new patterns

[25] Such a policy was recommended to the American government by the internationally known economist, Gottfried von Haberler. Although it was not officially adopted, it had numerous advocates in the U.S. administration before the sharpening international currency crisis in August 1971.

of behavior of the countries concerned must also be tried out. These reforms would oust the United States from its position of hegemony. At the beginning of 1972, the internationally renowned American economist Henry C. Wallich stated that for a long period of time the United States had gained considerable advantages from the reserve function of the dollar. However, the world is no longer willing to concede these advantages to the United States, and America itself is also no longer keen on them, since the cheaply financed deficits finally led to an intolerable overevaluation of the dollar. And shortly before the 1973 World Monetary Conference in Nairobi the same author wrote in an article for the September 7 issue of the *Frankfurter Allgemeine Zeitung*: "Basically, the American wishes and goals can be reduced to a common denominator: The United States advocates a monetary system which, in one way or another, would accomplish the same as the traditional dollar standard." Thus it becomes apparent that the United States attaches great importance to the loss of its monetary hegemony in the transatlantic dialogue.

In mid-1973 West German Minister of Finance (now Chancellor) Helmut Schmidt expressed the view that despite certain approximations of viewpoints there existed substantial differences of interest and opinion on important issues between Europe and the United States, differences which basically continued after the Nairobi conference. The bulletin of the Press and Information Service of the federal government in Bonn quoted him on June 2, 1973, as saying:

It is true, there is a certain degree of uniformity with a view to the future role of the special drawing rights as a main reserve instrument in place of the U.S. dollar; but what shall happen with the glut of dollars? Is it going to be consolidated and, if so, by whom, when, to what extent and under which conditions? What will happen to the gold as a traditional currency reserve in the central banks of many countries? How can one define the special drawing rights into which all currencies can be converted since they are an instrument of liquidity only between the central banks and the IMF? Who is to decide, and according to which criteria, on the creation of special drawing rights? Should they really serve purposes of development financing as well? Furthermore, by virtue of what kind of regulations shall the surplus and/or the deficit countries be induced to adjust either their general economic policies or their exchange rates? Shall controls of capital movements be permitted? In which instances? Shall there be a harmonization of the levels of interest rates? Finally, what kind of sanctions shall be provided for? By whom are they to be applied? By the IMF? But who is then the decision-making body of the IMF? Will a big country also yield to an IMF decision? Will the United States help to restore the authority of the IMF after it had substantially contributed to its curtailment?

The listing of some significant questions indicates the whole range of potential monetary conflicts.

Problems of Trade Policy

The controversy over various trade practices between the two partners of the Western alliance is of long standing. However, the economic conflicts have constantly increased in the past four years.

The European Community's objections to U.S. trade practices in the fields of tariff and nontariff trade barriers are countered by the United States' severe condemnation of the protectionist agricultural policy of the European Community. In addition, the policies of association and preferential treatment practiced by the European Community in its relations with the Mediterranean countries in Africa are subject to sharp criticism since the United States is of the opinion that they markedly increase the regionalization of world trade at U.S. expense.[26] Great Britain's entry into the European Community has extended its influence to the former British colonies. Therefore, on account of the special relations with the former French, Belgian and British possessions, an enormous sphere of interest of the European Community is developing in Africa.

By submitting the new trade law which incorporates numerous protectionist escape clauses, the U.S. administration clearly demonstrates the growing significance it attaches to economic policy within the overall context of American foreign policy. After the cease-fire agreement in Vietnam and the general disengagement of the United States in Asia, and backed by the newly established relations with the Soviet Union and, above all, with the People's Republic of China, the United States turns more and more in the direction of worldwide integration endeavors. Those in influential U.S. political circles regard the European unification as a political relief. This is the reason why the integration and expansion of the European Community are welcome, since they constitute an effective counterweight to the Eastern countries.[27]

But for some time this development has been increasingly considered to be a challenge disadvantageous to the U.S. economy. Along

[26] See K. Grimm and H. Hansenpflug, "Die handelspolitische Kontroverse EWG-USA," *Wirtschaftsdienst*, Apr. 1973, p. 187.

[27] See R. Dahrendorf, "Möglichkeiten und Grenzen einer Aussenpolitik der Europäischen Gemeinschaften," *Europa-Archiv*, Apr. 1971, p. 118.

with the deterioration in competitiveness, which increasingly applies also to high-quality technological products, the United States fears that, in the long run, it might forfeit the power upon which its supremacy was based and which has been the material basis of the American engagement in Western Europe. The course of unifying foreign policy decisions within the European Community is being energetically pursued. In particular, the task performed by the ambassadors of the member states in third countries will be increasingly coordinated. From the results of the consultations held so far—measured by the reactions in third countries—it becomes apparent that the newly acquired political identity of the European Community is highly valued by third parties. Cooperation with the European Community is widely considered a solution to the dilemma of choosing between the two superpowers. Above all, it is the policy of preferences pursued by the European Community toward the Mediterranean area in the Middle East which is expected to lead to an expansion of its territorial influence sphere. The introduction of a global Mediterranean policy is designed to establish a customs union or a free trade area within the Mediterranean region. As for the European Mediterranean countries, whose political structures resemble those of the EC countries and whose industries have reached an adequate level of development, the possibility of entry should be left open. During the past decade, economic ties were established which in the future might call in question the political and economic reasons for American and Soviet presence in this area. Dahrendorf has said that the European Community itself wishes to "contribute to a long-term stability."[28] This means working toward relations that will further an intensified economic intercourse, that is, economic modernization, and, at the same time, will safeguard an adequate, stable form of government. Thus the European community consciously joins the superpowers in their competition for the political molding of the world. Therefore, it does not come as a surprise that the great powers should make remarkable efforts to influence the European Community's organized common foreign policies.

There are still other economic problems which might lead to serious difficulties. Should the energy supply become as critical as anticipated by many experts, a lack of cooperation on the part of the consumer countries could result in a greater number of controversial issues between the United States and Europe. But even if this

28 Ibid., p. 128.

should not come about, the question will arise as to whether Europe is in danger of having the United States take advantage of European dependence on American nuclear protection in order to obtain unilateral economic concessions.

From an American point of view, this possibility cannot be excluded. However, according to Henry Kissinger, the recently increasing speculations concerning substantial disparities of views are largely unjustified. The presently parallel developing processes should be kept apart: European integration, the debate on organizing security within the framework of NATO, and—in a way overlying all these problems—the revised definition of the Atlantic relations, pursuant to Kissinger's original suggestions, in the form of a "New Atlantic Charter." In Kissinger's view, the discussions among European countries that have taken place in recent months have created a far-reaching conformity of views. Therefore the United States, which in the postwar period has persistently advocated the formation of a "European identity," considered the September 27, 1973, declaration of the Nine an important initial attempt of the European allies to adopt a concerted stance with regard to the political reshaping of Atlantic relations. At the same time, Kissinger expressed the view that the United States would have to reserve its right to present its own views in further negotiations. Washington's proposals should not be regarded in terms of a "take-it-or-leave-it" attitude, but as a basis for a free discussion among partners.

Summing up, we can note that in our times economic policy has a decisive impact on foreign policy, and that economic factors can even constitute a significant reason for foreign policy developments. We can also say that elements of national economics are turned into instruments of foreign policy. Let us think, for instance, of crude oil and of the possibly dangerous effect that the quest for energy resources might have on decisions in foreign affairs. Today's world is getting smaller and smaller. The times when, as Goethe says in *Faust*, "in Turkey or lands far away . . . malcontents have unleashed the dogs of war, . . . while in Europe people could go for their peaceful Easter stroll," have long since passed. There is no event in any spot of the world which could not cause its waves to flood all over our planet. Space has become smaller; particles in space collide ever more. Thousands of new problems arise daily. However, we are also becoming aware of the fact that we, people of all races, nations, and creeds, must live together. May we draw from this awareness hope for lasting peace?

Participants

ROBERT A. BAUER is Director of the Kenyon Public Affairs Forum and Adjunct Professor of Political Science, Kenyon College. He also serves as United States Representative of the Organization for International Economic Relations, Vienna, and as a lecturer-consultant for the United States Information Agency. He is a retired Senior Officer of the United States Foreign Service.

FRITZ BOCK is Chairman of the Board, Creditanstalt–Bankverein, and President of the Organization for International Economic Relations, Vienna. He is a former Austrian Vice Chancellor and Minister for Trade and Reconstruction.

RONALD CLIFTON is Economics Affairs Officer, Middle East, South Asia, and North Africa, and Country Desk Officer for India, Sri Lanka, and Nepal, United States Information Agency. He was Resident Economic Specialist of the United States Information Service in India and Director of the American University Center in Calcutta.

DOROTHY CROOK is Senior Editor of *Economic Impact*, a quarterly publication of the United States Information Agency published in English and Spanish and distributed abroad. She was Press Officer for Economic Affairs of the U.S. Mission to the United Nations, Executive Director of the U.S. Committee for the United Nations, and Economics Editor for the Voice of America.

EDWIN L. DALE, JR., is Economic Writer for the *New York Times*. He was the *Times*'s European Economic Correspondent in London and a reporter and editorial writer for the *New York Herald Tribune* in Washington. He has been a contributor to the *London Economist* and is the author of *Conservatives in Politics* (1960).

JAMES R. DICKENSON is a writer for the *National Observer* in Washington and has covered sports, Capitol Hill, and, since 1967, national politics, including the 1968 and 1972 presidential elections. He has contributed chapters to a number of anthologies. In 1973 he was nominated for a Pulitzer Prize for his coverage of Watergate.

Lewis A. Dunn, formerly Assistant Professor of Political Science, Kenyon College, is on the staff of the Hudson Institute, Croton-on-Hudson, New York.

Warren W. Eason is Director of Graduate Studies, Department of Economics, The Ohio State University. He was Assistant Professor of Economics, Princeton University; Associate Professor of Economics, Syracuse University; and Lecturer in Economics, Johns Hopkins University. He is the author of articles in the field of Soviet population and manpower development.

Frank L. Fernbach is Assistant to the President for Special Projects, United Steelworkers of America, Washington, D.C. He has held numerous positions in the labor movement, was a member of the U.S. delegation to UNESCO conferences, and has been on presidential commissions and task forces. He has been a contributor to various economic, labor, and educational journals.

Michael G. Finn is Research Associate for the Center for Human Resource Research, The Ohio State University. He has held various other teaching positions. His publications include: *Growth Patterns of a Region: Jackson County, Michigan*, with Donald Blome and David Milstein (1966); and *Education and the Labor Force in Ecuador: A Statistical Report*, with D. Hilsaca (1973).

John P. Hardt is Senior Specialist, Congressional Research Service, Library of Congress, and Professorial Lecturer in Economics, George Washington University. He has held various research and teaching positions and was a member of the congressional delegation to the Soviet Union, Poland, West Germany, and the United Kingdom. Among his publications are: *Soviet Economic Statistics*, with V. G. Treml (1972); *U.S.-Soviet Commercial Relations: The Interplay of Economics, Technology Transfer, and Diplomacy*, with George Holliday (1973); and *Soviet Economic Prospects in the Seventies* (1973).

John R. Karlik is International Economist, Joint Economic Committee, U.S. Congress. He was a member of the professional staff, Hudson Institute, Croton-on-Hudson, New York, and Economist in the Federal Reserve Bank of New York. He has contributed to a number of anthologies and journals.

Young C. Kim is Associate Professor of Political Science, George Washington University. He has held teaching and research positions at Hobart and William Smith colleges and at Vanderbilt University.

Among his publications are: *Major Issues in Japan's Security Policy Debate* (1969), *Japan's Security Policy toward Communist China* (1970), *Japan's Defense Policy* (1971), *Japan in World Politics* (1972), and *Major Powers and Korea* (1973).

EDWARD L. MORSE is Assistant Professor of Politics and International Affairs, Woodrow Wilson School of Public and International Affairs, Princeton University. He is the author of *A Comparative Approach to the Study of Foreign Policy: Notes on Theorizing* (1971), *Foreign Policy and Interdependence in Gaullist France* (1973), and numerous articles and reviews.

VLADIMIR PETROV is Professor of International Relations, George Washington University, teaching modern East European history and history of Soviet foreign policy. Among his publications are: *Soviet Historians and the German Invasion* (1969), *A Study in Diplomacy: The Story of Arthur Bliss Lane* (1971), and *Escape from the Future* (1973).

ALFRED PUHAN is Special Consultant to the President, Corn Production System, Inc., Chicago. He was American Ambassador to Hungary; Deputy Assistant Secretary of State for European Affairs; Minister, American Embassy, Bangkok; and Director of the Office of German Affairs, Department of State.

RICHARD H. ROVERE is Chairman of the Editorial Advisory Board of *Washington Monthly* and a staff writer for the *New Yorker*. He was Associate Editor, the *New Masses*, Assistant Editor, the *Nation*, and Editor, *Common Sense*. Among his numerous publications are: *Affairs of State: The Eisenhower Years* (1956), *Senator Joe McCarthy* (1959), *The Goldwater Caper* (1965), and *Waist Deep in the Big Muddy* (1968).

FRANK M. TAMAGNA is Professor of Economics, American University, Washington, D.C., and is an economic consultant to the World Bank, Washington, D.C., and to various central and commercial banks. His publications include: *Banking and Financing in China* (1942), *Central Banking in Latin America* (1962), and *Commercial Banking in the Modern Economy* (1972).

JAMES D. THEBERGE is Director of Latin American and Hispanic Studies at the Center for Strategic and International Studies, Georgetown University, Washington, D.C. He was an economic adviser to the U.S. Aid Mission to Argentina, and to the Inter-American Development Bank. He has been an economic consultant to the World Bank, the Inter-American Development Bank, the Andean Development Corporation, the United Nations, and various Latin American, African, and Far Eastern governments. His publications include: *The Economics of Trade and Development* (1968); *Soviet Seapower in the Caribbean: Political and Strategic Implications* (1972); *The Western Mediterranean: Political, Economic and Strategic Aspects,* with Alvin J. Cottrell (1973); and *Russia in the Caribbean* (1973).

RICHARD J. TRETHEWEY is Assistant Professor of Economics, Kenyon College. He was Visiting Instructor, M.B.A. Program, Seattle University. His articles have appeared in a number of publications.

HELEN W. H. YIN is Economist, Bureau of Economic Analysis, U.S. Department of Commerce. She was Assistant Professor of Asian Studies, University of Southern California. She is coauthor of *Economic Statistics of Mainland China* (1960).

RICHARD Y. C. YIN is Associate Professor of Economics and a member of the Institute for Sino-Soviet Studies, George Washington University. He taught economics at the University of Southern California and Wabash College, and was a Research Fellow in Chinese Economic Studies, Harvard University. He is coauthor of *Economic Statistics of Mainland China* (1960).